COUNSELLING AND PSYCHOTHERAPY IN ORGANISATIONAL SETTINGS

Other books in this series

What is Counselling & Psychotherapy?
by Norman Claringbull   ISBN 978 1 84445 361 0

Creating the Therapeutic Relationship in
Counselling and Psychotherapy by Judith Green   ISBN 978 1 84445 463 1

Reflective Practice in Counselling and
Psychotherapy by Sofie Bager-Charleson   ISBN 978 1 84445 360 3

Books in the Mental Health Practice series

Mental Health Law in England and Wales
by Paul Barber, Robert Brown and Debbie Martin   ISBN 978 1 84445 195 1

Cognitive Behavioural Interventions for Mental
Health Practitioners by Alec Grant   ISBN 978 1 84445 210 1

Child and Adolescent Mental Health: A Guide
for Practice by Steven Walker   ISBN 978 0 85725 057 5

To order, please contact our distributor: BEBC Distribution, Albion Close,
Parkstone, Poole, BH12 3LL. Telephone 0845 230 9000,
email: **learningmatters@bebc.co.uk**. You can also find more
information on each of these titles and our other learning resources at
www.learningmatters.co.uk

Want to write for the Counselling and Psychotherapy Practice series? Contact the
Commissioning Editor, Luke Block (Luke@learningmatters.co.uk), with your ideas
and proposals.

COUNSELLING AND PSYCHOTHERAPY IN ORGANISATIONAL SETTINGS

EDITED BY JUDY MOORE AND RUTH ROBERTS

Series editor: Norman Claringbull

LearningMatters

First published in 2010 by Learning Matters Ltd

British Library Cataloguing in Publication Data
A CIP record for this book is available from the British Library.

ISBN: 978 1 84445 614 7

This book is also available in the following ebook formats:

Adobe ebook	ISBN: 978 1 84445 767 0
EPUB ebook	ISBN: 978 1 84445 766 3
Kindle	ISBN: 978 0 85725 024 7

1006336769

Cover design by Code 5 Design Associates
Project management by Diana Chambers
Typeset by Kelly Winter
Printed and bound in Great Britain by TJ International, Padstow, Cornwall

Learning Matters Ltd
33 Southernhay East
Exeter EX1 1NX
Tel: 01392 215560
info@learningmatters.co.uk
www.learningmatters .co.uk

FSC
Mixed Sources
Product group from well-managed
forests and other controlled sources
Cert no. SGS-COC-2482
www.fsc.org
© 1996 Forest Stewardship Council

Contents

Series Editor's Preface

It does not seem to matter whether you are a newcomer to counselling and psychotherapy or an old hand; getting an understanding of what the talking therapies are all about is not easy. On the theoretical side, there is an overwhelming assortment of counselling and psychotherapy approaches on offer. Which ones should newly emerging therapists adopt? When and where should they use them? This can be a puzzle for experienced therapists too. On the practical side, trainee therapists are inevitably first taught their clinical skills against a limited range of classroom exercises and work experience placements. Will those skills suit their eventual clients?

These sorts of difficulties might leave some therapists with daunting challenges. How can they use and adapt any newly learned skills, or any original training, to suit the real-life practical circumstances that they now find themselves working in? These are real-world questions that real-world practitioners have to answer. So, if these sorts of issues are puzzling you too, then do not worry – they puzzle everyone. The good news is that in this book some very experienced practitioners will tell you how they have worked out some very useful, very practical, real-life answers to these sorts of posers.

'What do therapists actually do?' is the question that everybody asks, be they potential trainees or potential clients. Probably the easiest way to tackle this question is to rephrase it. What do different types of therapists do? Under what sorts of circumstances do they do it? Helping you to answer those questions is what this book is all about. 'Newbie' therapists will want to know if their initial training will qualify them to work wherever they get appointed. The reality is that in some cases it might and in other cases it might not. However, what their training will certainly do, will be to provide them with a useful foundation from which they can begin to build and to adapt their evolving skills as circumstances dictate. Gaining an understanding of the varying professional demands placed on the average therapist is also what this book is all about. It does this by telling you what it is like working in some of the more well-known types of counselling and psychotherapy services. Further, it describes the realities of everyday life for therapists working in those services – it tells you what they do and it also tells you how they do it.

This is a practical book for practical therapists. One view of counselling and psychotherapy is that it is, at base, a purposeful activity. In other words, trainee therapists are not learning for learning's sake – they are learning in order to apply their knowledge to the real world about them. This is the concept of *praxis* – the testing of theory in real situations and then amending it according to experience. That is exactly what all the contributors to this book have done.

Counselling and psychotherapy can often be a lonely calling. Many therapists work by themselves or with just with one or two colleagues. Of course, every therapist is essentially alone when finally sitting down in the consulting room with a client. However, today's emerging therapists do not have to be alone in the sense that many of their professional colleagues are already on the same journey. Therapists do not have to be explorers of new lands. Maps and travellers' guides are available and you will find some very useful therapeutic 'road maps' in this book.

All of the contributors to this book are experienced practitioners. They all have extensive professional knowledge of the various institutions and settings that they have written about. You will find explanatory theory, practical lessons and professional guidance throughout the book which includes reflection points, research summaries, guided discussion topics, case studies and suggestions for further reading. In the following chapters you will find the most up-to-date information about how counselling and psychotherapy can, and indeed should, be delivered when it is provided as part of a dedicated therapy service, institution or professional setting. The rest is up to you.

The editors of this book, Judy Moore and Ruth Roberts, are both knowledgeable teachers and practitioners of counselling and psychotherapy and they have made sure that some of the most important working sectors for the practising therapist have been explored. What is it like being a counsellor or a psychotherapist working in the education sector? What are the roles of counsellors working in the voluntary sector or in residential settings? Do psychotherapists in prisons or in occupational health need their own specialist knowledge and particular skills? All of these issues, and more, are examined, not just in theory but also in practice, in the pages that follow.

If you want to know how real people do real counselling, then this is the book for you. It tells you how some well-respected, well-established practitioners do what they do. Even better, it tells you how you can do it too.

Dr Norman Claringbull – Series Editor
www.normanclaringbull.co.uk

Acknowledgements

This book would not have been possible without the willingness of all the contributing counsellors and psychotherapists, many of them local colleagues, to write openly about their own experiences of engaging in therapeutic work in their respective organisational contexts. We thank all of them for their cooperation and goodwill in participating in this project.

We are grateful to all colleagues at the University of East Anglia, Norwich, for making our own working context a particularly congenial one. We are fortunate in knowing that our work is valued within the institution and we acknowledge the contribution of all our immediate colleagues – both counsellors and admin staff – to the Counselling Service's reputation.

We thank Luke Block and Lauren Simpson of Learning Matters for their encouragement and supportive editing.

Judy Moore and Ruth Roberts

About the contributors

Fredrick Asare is a Counselling Psychologist in training, currently completing his doctoral training at City University, London. He has worked as a high intensity therapist at the IAPT site in the South Essex Partnership NHS Foundation Trust (SEPT) since its inception in 2009. Before working in the IAPT he gained several years' experience working in various NHS primary and secondary care services. Fredrick's research interests are concerned with readjustment issues among military populations following active duty in combat.

Cathy Austin has been a counsellor and psychotherapist for 25 years. She is currently the Director of Counselling at the St Barnabas Counselling Centre and is the counsellor for students at Norwich City College. She is particularly interested in dissociative disorders, recovery from childhood trauma and adolescent angst.

Norman Claringbull is the former Head of Counselling and Psychotherapy Studies at Southampton University. He currently combines his commercial consultancy work and private practice with ongoing research and various academic appointments at a number of UK universities. Norman is also Series Editor for Counselling and Psychotherapy Practice by Learning Matters.

Judy Moore is Director of the University Counselling Service and Director of the Centre for Counselling Studies at the University of East Anglia. She trained as a counsellor in the mid-1980s and has worked in student counselling since then. Throughout much of the 1990s she was a core tutor on the UEA postgraduate diploma in counselling and has subsequently taught on the Centre's diploma in focusing and experiential psychotherapy as well as supervising counselling research students. She is particularly interested in how cultural and contextual factors impact upon counselling process.

Paul O'Sullivan is a Counselling Psychologist in training, currently completing his doctoral training at City University, London. He has worked as a high intensity therapist at the IAPT site in the South Essex Partnership NHS Foundation Trust (SEPT) since its inception in 2009. Before working in the IAPT he gained several years' experience working in various NHS primary and secondary care services. Paul's research activities have focused on the impact of speech impediments on social interactions, particularly on the process of forming new relationships.

Frank Paice qualified as a counsellor in 1999 after a career in education. He has built successful practices, based in the centre of Norwich and in rural south Norfolk. He sees a mixture of clients and supervisees from across East Anglia, as well as providing clinical supervision for health professionals outside counselling. A significant number of Frank's clients are NHS employees who are referred by their occupational health service. He has also worked extensively for employee assistance programmes.

Ruth Roberts is a BACP accredited counsellor and Deputy Director of the Counselling Service at the University of East Anglia. Ruth has a background in Higher Education administration and, after completing her MA in counselling at UEA, began working there as Educational Counsellor in 2006. Ruth's main interest is in working with and researching the emotional aspects of learning and addressing disaffection among university students.

Steve Roberts trained in Person Centred Counselling at UEA before completing his master's degree focusing on addiction. He followed his initial qualification with training in Cognitive Behavioural Therapy, which now underpins much of his work as Lead Therapist and Clinic Manager for Priory Healthcare in Norwich. He now works with clients with a range of mental and emotional disorders as well as addiction. Steve's experience as an addictions therapist in a residential treatment centre continues to inform his practice. His interest in addiction also informs his current PhD research into attitudinal factors which influence patients' progress in treatment.

Kelvin Smith joined the St Barnabas Counselling Centre, Norwich, in August 2002. He had taken early retirement the year before from British Telecom where he had held a variety of posts with the company since 1966. His background was mainly in electrical engineering and contract supervision but he had spent time in a planning department and as a technical support adviser in resource management. He considers himself a 'Jack of all trades and master of none', which has given him all the organisational tools needed for the post of administrator at the St Barnabas Counselling Centre.

Gwen Spall trained as an integrative counsellor, with a strong person-centred foundation. She is accredited with the Association of Christian Counsellors and specialises in working with adolescents. After five years as school counsellor at one of Norfolk's largest high schools, Gwen has recently reduced her schools counselling work to become Norfolk County Council's Restorative Approaches Co-ordinator. She has always had a keen interest in teenage emotional health, previously running a project in Norwich on the dangers of child sexual exploitative relationships. She also works from home, counselling in private practice.

Introduction

Judy Moore and Ruth Roberts

Counselling and Psychotherapy in Organisational Settings was conceived in response to ongoing developments in the world of counselling and psychotherapy. We were aware that many counsellors and psychotherapists enter the workplace with little or no awareness of the likely impact on their work of the broader organisation in which counselling takes place. Counselling and psychotherapy training, whatever the orientation of that training, usually majors in the one-to-one therapeutic encounter. While contextual factors such as class, race and gender may be considered as part of training, little attention is generally given to how the immediate organisational context may impact – both positively and negatively – on counselling work. Yet the reality is that most counsellors, at some time in their working lives, will work within an organisation. There is an increasing diversity of public and private organisations where counselling and psychotherapy are embedded as part of the provision to employees and service users and counselling is already embedded in many educational establishments. In recognition of the need for deeper understanding of organisational issues, the British Association for Counselling and Psychotherapy (BACP) now requires 50 hours 'work-based learning' in addition to placement hours for accredited counselling courses (2009). Although the new course accreditation requirements will not be implemented until 2014, courses are increasingly introducing projects and assignments that require trainees to consider the context and practices of a typical counselling service.

Some counsellors and psychotherapists might argue that, even within organisations, counselling and psychotherapy should take place within a vacuum of confidentiality that provides clients with a neutral, safe place in which to voice their concerns. However, in practice, many counsellors and psychotherapists working in organisational settings find that the needs of the client have to be finely balanced with the interests of the organisation as a whole. These competing interests can raise some interesting and taxing concerns for practitioners who are usually working within strict budgetary restraints and with an awareness of the overarching aims and mission of the organisation. The aim of this book is to illustrate how many counsellors and psychotherapists grapple with these issues on a day-to-day basis and how an awareness of the contextual setting of practice can actually enhance the service that is offered to clients.

This book is aimed at experienced and trainee counsellors and psycho-therapists alike. Readers who are currently in training will find the book useful on many levels, whether applying for training placements or undertaking the work-based learning elements of their course. For the experienced practitioner, we hope this book will offer an insight into different sectors in which counselling and psychotherapy are embedded and provide valuable background information for individuals applying for new posts in organisational settings. For others, already working in the settings described here, we hope the book will enable reflection on current practice and a chance to understand better the counsellor's role in organ-isational settings.

SOME GENERAL POINTS TO NOTE

Counselling in an organisational setting may or may not be workplace coun-selling. Several texts address issues involved in counselling in the workplace (e.g. Carroll, 1996; Coles, 2001; Berridge and Cooper, 2004; Franklin, 2003; Bryant-Jefferies, 2005) and a comprehensive review of research in this area have been drawn together (McLeod, 2008). Less has been written about the broader organisational context and this book endeavours to acknowledge the fact that voluntary organisations, educational establishments and residential settings face many of the issues that also confront those who offer counselling to employees in the workplace. Trainee counsellors on placement suddenly find themselves in a context where they are highly trained in one-to-one interpersonal interaction but are totally ignorant of organisational dynamics and institutional pressures under which they may be working.

Carroll and Walton cite McLeod's list of challenges faced by counsellors working in non-counselling organisations:

- being pressured to produce results desired by the agency rather than the client;
- maintaining confidential boundaries;
- justifying the cost of the service;
- dealing with isolation;
- educating colleagues about the purpose and value of counselling;
- justifying the cost of supervision;
- avoiding being overwhelmed by numbers of clients, or becoming the conscience of the organisation;
- avoiding the threat to reputation caused by 'failure' cases;
- coping with the envy of colleagues who are not able to take an hour for each client interview;
- creating an appropriate office space and reception system.
    (McLeod, 1993, p273; quoted in Carroll and Walton, 1997, p18)

These challenges are common to all contexts covered in the following chapters, even including the voluntary sector where trustees are likely to scrutinise the work of the counselling agency for which they hold financial responsibility.

The paradox of counselling and psychotherapy training in the UK to date is that scant attention has been given to where the work for which individuals are being so intensively trained will actually take place. Several factors are now, however, inviting a more rigorous approach to this aspect of our work.

A RESPONSE TO ONGOING DEVELOPMENTS: REGULATION OF COUNSELLING AND PSYCHOTHERAPY

In February 2007, the British government published a White Paper entitled *Trust, Assurance and Safety – The Regulation of Health Professionals in the 21st Century*, which stated that:

- *7.2 The Government is planning to introduce statutory regulation for applied psychologists, psychotherapists and counsellors and other psychological therapists. . .*

- *7.16 Psychologists, psychotherapists and counsellors will be regulated by the Health Professions Council following that Council's rigorous process of assessing their regulatory needs and ensuring that its system is capable of accommodating them. This will be the first priority for future regulation.*

The BACP defines regulation in the following terms.

> *Statutory regulation means that a profession is regulated by an independent council that does not belong to any professional body or interest group. In regulating a profession a professional title is protected. Then it is only people who are registered to use that title can legally refer to themselves by it.*
> **(www.bacp.co.uk/regulation/regulationFAQ.php)**

One of the primary implications of regulation is the standardisation of training and core competencies for entry into the professions of Counselling and Psychotherapy. Under current proposals, Counselling and Psychotherapy will be separate titles on the register and will thus have some variation in the core competencies identified for each role. Practitioners currently accredited as counsellors and psychotherapists will most likely be able to enter the register on both strands, while new entrants may need to decide prior to commencing their training under which title they would like to register. In practice, however, many training institutions are likely to provide comprehensive training courses that encompass the core competencies for both titles. It is with this in mind that this book addresses both counsellors and psychotherapists alike (and those who use both titles in their professional work).

The philosophical and practical issues currently being debated in the Health Professions Council (HPC) consultation on statutory regulation are wide ranging and sometimes evoke passionate responses. There is not scope in this Introduction to address these issues fully. However, it is important to note that regulation provides an important backdrop to the book and may bring about important changes to the way in which Counselling and Psychotherapy are presented to the public (both in the use of titles and in the employment of practitioners). From our perspective, the single most important implication of regulation will be on the training of counsellors and psychotherapists, and the increased requirement for work-based learning in accredited courses preparing trainees to meet the core competencies for regulation.

IMPLICATIONS FOR TRAINING

Counselling training is usually undertaken within the context of a particular theoretical approach (or integrated approaches) whereby the primary focus is on the encounter between client and counsellor. Emphasis is usually placed on the counsellor's own growth and development in preparation for the challenges of practice at the interpersonal level of the counselling process. Paradoxically, it was only in the early years of the development of counselling in the UK that context-specific training took place, through courses in student counselling established at the Universities of Aston (1971) and London (1972). Since then, training has become shaped more by the definitions of the theoretical approach.

Increasingly, however, counsellors find themselves working in a variety of institutional settings where counselling practice is determined not only by the counsellor's theoretical approach but by the philosophy, culture and economic boundaries of the institution. Additionally, wider social and economic pressures are increasingly at the forefront of policy decisions with regard to the nation's mental health and emotional well-being. Every counsellor, therefore, whether starting out or managing changes in the workplace, needs a thorough understanding of these contextual challenges to practice.

In addition to these developments, as noted above, the introduction of statutory regulation is likely to have important implications for training. The BACP has already responded to this likely future development by publishing a new 'Core Curriculum', popularly known as the 'Gold Book' (2009), with an increased requirement for work-based learning of 50 hours in addition to a training placement of 150 client hours.

The BACP defines work-based learning as:

> *[presenting] students with opportunities to explore and gain contextual awareness in a professional counselling and/or psychotherapy or appropriate related setting. The learning experience should be designed to enable students to relate their training to the workplace.*
>
> *Such opportunities for work-based learning might typically include clerical duties; attending team meetings; case management conferences; reading literature, policies and procedures; skills practice; structured training; observation, assisting, mentoring or job shadowing . . .*

(BACP, 2009, p12)

We hope that *Counselling and Psychotherapy in Organisational Settings* will provide a useful training resource to lecturers and students regarding these elements of their course as well as providing practical advice and insight for qualified practitioners preparing for accreditation or regulation in the future.

Implementation of the 'Gold Book' has been delayed from its original launch date of 2011 to 2014. In the meantime, courses are adapting themselves to the new requirements and there is likely to be a gradual phasing-in of work-based learning between now and 2014. Courses are re-accredited on a five-year cycle and those that come up for review between now and 2014 will need to accommodate the new work-based learning requirements.

ACCREDITATION

Most counsellors working in organisational settings will be accredited either by BACP, the Confederation of Scottish Counselling Agencies (COSCA), the United Kingdom Council for Psychotherapy (UKCP) or an equivalent professional body. For the purposes of this Introduction we will focus on BACP requirements as they exemplify the need for practice-based learning.

Accreditation by a professional body will be a requirement under statutory regulation and advertisements for counsellors in any organisational setting are likely to include a statement that applicants should either be accredited or 'working towards accreditation'. Current BACP requirements state that the applicant should be a member of BACP, covered by professional indemnity insurance, be in current practice, with a minimum 1.5 hours of supervision per month, and have met the training requirements, which include 450 hours of supervised practice, at least 150 of which must be undertaken after the completion of training.

It is this last requirement that most impacts on counselling in organisational settings. All counsellors-in-training and their newly qualified colleagues need placements. Counsellors are discouraged from taking private clients during and immediately after their training period and most counsellors will work on a voluntary basis to achieve most, if not all, of their qualifying 450 hours. Their services are increasingly sought by organisations which are under constant pressure, particularly in the current economic climate, to provide more counselling with fewer resources.

Despite this requirement, it is interesting to note that the current 'reflective practice' criteria for accreditation do not invite reflection on workplace or organisational issues:

> *8.1 Knowledge and understanding*
> *8.1.1   Describe a rationale for your client work with reference to the theory/ theories that inform your practice.*
> *8.1.2   Describe the place of your self-awareness within your way of working.*
> *8.1.3   Describe how issues of difference and equality impact upon the therapeutic relationship.*
>
> **(www.bacp.co.uk/accreditation)**

It is interesting to speculate how this aspect of the criteria might change in the light of the new 'Gold Book' requirements. Our hypothesis is that 'knowledge and understanding' of organisational context is likely to be included in the future.

ETHICS

All of the counsellors and psychotherapists who have contributed to this book work to the ethical guidelines of their professional body. In recent years, 'codes' of ethics have been replaced by a less rigid 'Framework', which invites the practitioner to reflect on the competing pressures under which they are operating. In addition to the BACP Ethical Framework criteria for 'Providing a Good Standard of Practice and Care', of 'Keeping Trust' (criteria 11–19) and 'Respecting Privacy and Confidentiality' (20–4), which are common to all counselling practice, the criteria that most impact on the organisational setting, and present some of the challenges to counsellors outlined in the chapters below, are 'Awareness of Context' (56) and 'Making and Receiving Referrals' (57 and 58).

In terms of 'Context', the Ethical Framework suggests that the practitioner *is responsible for learning about and taking account of the different protocols, conventions and customs that can pertain to different working contexts and cultures* (BACP, 2010, p9). In terms of 'Making and Receiving Referrals' the criteria for ethical practice are as follows:

57. All routine referrals to colleagues and other services should be discussed with the client in advance and the client's consent obtained both to making the referral and also to disclosing information to accompany the referral. Reasonable care should be taken to ensure that:

- *the recipient of the referral is able to provide the required service;*
- *any confidential information disclosed during the referral process will be adequately protected;*
- *the referral will be likely to benefit the client.*

58. Prior to accepting a referral the practitioner should give careful consideration to:

- *the appropriateness of the referral;*
- *the likelihood that the referral will be beneficial to the client;*
- *the adequacy of the client's consent for the referral.*

If the referrer is professionally required to retain overall responsibility for the work with the client, it is considered to be professionally appropriate to provide the referrer with brief progress reports. Such reports should be made in consultation with clients and not normally against their explicit wishes.
(BACP, 2010, p9)

The chapters in this book engage with the complexities of how the need for referral or collaboration can arise and some of the ways in which the institution or organisation can work with any client and their counsellor towards the best possible outcome. The need to work ethically is always paramount for counsellors and it is their responsibility to make clear the limits of their communication outside the counselling room, to be aware of when communication with other parts of the organisation can be helpful or where it can amount to a breach of the client's trust.

CHAPTER OVERVIEW

There are eight chapters in this book, each written by experienced practitioners active in their field. The organisational settings chosen here were considered to be sectors where counselling and psychotherapy have an established presence and where many counsellors and psychotherapists find employment or placements. In some instances, such as Occupational Health and Improving Access to Psychological Therapies (IAPT), the nature and role of counselling and psychotherapy are relatively new, and are continuing to be established and defined. In all settings, however, the roles of counselling and psychotherapy are under constant review and the shifting nature of the profession is something that underpins the focus of the book. Readers will understand the need to be responsive to changes in policy and regulation that affect practitioners in different fields. In addition, each author has provided a background to the field in which they work and an overview of the current issues facing counsellors and psychotherapists in their day-to-day work.

The first three chapters focus on counselling in educational settings: schools, Further Education and Higher Education. In these chapters we see how the educational setting can be both a focus and backdrop to the therapeutic work. In her chapter on counselling in schools, Gwen Spall considers the wider role of the counsellor in informing educational practice with an exploration of new initiatives in schools such as introducing restorative justice for conflict resolution. In the chapters on Further and Higher Education we see the effects of funding on counselling provision and the need for counselling services to clearly and continually define their purpose and role in these sectors. Chapter 4 gives an overview of working in the voluntary sector. Many trainees find placements in this sector and this chapter gives valuable insight into the qualities required to work in a sector where many people are unpaid yet remain committed to professional ideals and standards. Chapters 5 and 6 provide an insight into counselling and psychotherapy in settings where clients are either incarcerated (in prison) or in residential treatment for addictions. There are specific and difficult challenges facing practitioners in these settings with regard to the nature of the client group, the physical setting of the work and the tasks of the role. In particular, the therapist in a residential setting may be required to develop several strings to his or her bow in addition to one-to-one therapy. Chapters 7 and 8 focus on areas where counselling and psychotherapy are undergoing development and redefinition. Frank Paice's chapter on Counselling for Employee Assistance Programmes and in Occupational Health settings draws out the different influences and stakeholders in the counselling process and the need to work with an awareness of, and sensitivity to, these interests. Chapter 8 focuses on the newest development in counselling and psychotherapy; that of the Increasing Access to Psychological Therapies (IAPT) agenda introduced by the Labour government in 2006. The focus of this chapter is on the professional structure of this new sector of work and the challenge to practitioners working within tightly defined roles.

As you will see, the weighting of chapters varies throughout the book. Some chapters are heavily referenced due to the availability of literature and research in these fields – for example, the chapters 'Counselling and psycho-therapy in prisons' and 'Addictions counselling in a residential treatment centre'. Others, however, have few external references as there is currently little information or research on counselling and psychotherapy in these fields. In particular, there were few external resources for Chapter 4, 'Counselling in a voluntary agency', and Chapter 2 'Counselling in Further Education'. These chapters draw heavily on the contributors' experiences of working in these fields and highlight avenues for future research into the effectiveness and role of counselling and psychotherapy in such sectors. All chapters draw on the contributors' hands-on experience of working in their chosen field(s) and this factor gives a unique emphasis to the book, providing what we hope will be useful personal insight as well as academic analysis.

CHAPTER 1

Counselling in schools

Gwen Spall

CORE KNOWLEDGE

- Counselling in schools normally means counselling in a secondary school, working with the 11–18 age group.
- Adolescents are at a particular developmental stage, which needs empathic handling.
- There are other services, individuals and frameworks that need to be considered and worked within.
- The *Every Child Matters* (ECM) agenda places duties of care on schools that go far beyond mere academic achievement.
- Confidentiality, child protection, disclosure, parental consent and working with those at risk need careful consideration and navigation, particularly while bearing in mind that those you will be working with are under 18.
- Restorative approaches, particularly if applied to the whole school setting, can have an enormous impact.
- Working creatively is essential for school-based work.

INTRODUCTION

In this chapter the reader will learn and understand some of the complexities of working with adolescents in a school setting, specifically:

- the need to work creatively;
- the nature of, and ability to address, physical practicalities;
- issues around disclosure;
- safeguarding;
- contracting;
- the Common Assessment Framework (CAF);
- restorative approaches;
- routes in.

School counselling in the UK increasingly takes place in the context of secondary education and involves working with 11–16-year-olds. It might also include working with 16–18-year-olds where the school has a sixth form.

One definition of the role of a school counsellor is as follows:

> *Counselling is an interaction in a therapeutic setting, focusing primarily on a conversation about relationships, beliefs and behaviour (including feelings), through which the child's perceived problem is elucidated and framed or reframed in a fitting way, and in which new solutions are generated and the problem takes on new meaning.*
>
> (Bor, 2002, p15)

Teaching as a profession is necessarily very structured and goal oriented. Subjects must be studied methodically to realise exam success. Counselling is quite different, usually with no specific agenda on the part of the adult professional. A structured, cognitive, tools-based approach might appear to fit in a school setting, and might be more easily understood by teaching staff. However, an integrative approach, with a strong person-centred foundation, has become my preferred model.

Young clients occasionally appear to expect the counsellor to wave a magic wand and to find solutions to their problems and inevitably they will be disappointed. I have a strong sense that young people, especially in a school setting, expect to be directed. However, counselling in this setting provides many instances for the counsellor to be led by the 'magic' that goes on in the client as the counsellor trusts in their actualising tendency – that is, the client's ability to seek to fulfil their potential for growth.

Carl Rogers aptly described this in terms of a bucket of potatoes, placed in an attic. The potatoes will naturally shoot and grow towards any available light. In the counselling room it may not always look like this is what is happening and there may be times when it also feels that it is not, but this is when the counsellor needs to trust their client. In a very directive environment it can easily feel as though you are travelling in a distinctively different direction from everyone else. This, too, is part of the complexity of working in school: one may well work alone as the sole counsellor in a sea of professionals who more or less understand each other and their way of working. And while there may be other professionals to whom one might make referrals, they are generally not available for corridor chats or to bounce ideas off. Supervision, therefore, becomes a lifeline as the counsellor may well feel isolated in the school environment.

Other peculiarities to the school setting include dealing with issues of parental consent, child protection, safeguarding and the recently introduced

CAF. Working in a school setting as a counsellor is a little like being part of a jigsaw. The whole issue of confidentiality needs thorough grounding within the school before the implementation of a counselling service. Finding a place within the pastoral system where counselling might sit is not a task for the faint-hearted. The government's restorative approaches agenda (discussed in more detail later in this chapter) also dovetails into a school counselling role and has potential for enormous impact on a school ethos.

The presenting problems that recur in a school setting are issues around parental separation, bereavement, self-injury, drug and alcohol use, sexual abuse, self-esteem, peer relationships, bullying and boy/girl relationships. Occasionally, the counsellor may encounter issues around school work-related stress, but generally the issues tend to be very personal to the individual.

SCHOOL COUNSELLING: A RATIONALE

The Children Act 2004, the official stamp of the ECM agenda, places a duty on agencies working with children to co-operate in order to improve children's well-being. This agenda is nowhere more keenly reinforced than within a school community. The Office for Standards in Education (OFSTED) will look closely at a school's commitment to this framework and how closely students are supported pastorally. Long gone are the years of schools as exclusively educational establishments.

The ECM agenda identifies five main outcomes for children, and the Children's Plan 2020 Goals, released in April 2008, align some ambitious objectives with the original five outcomes. These outcomes sit very comfortably within a counselling role. As a result, many schools choose to develop their pastoral team to include such professionals as counsellors.

The five main outcomes are that children and young people should:

- be healthy – mentally, emotionally and sexually, and able to choose not to use illegal drugs;
- stay safe – from maltreatment, neglect, violence, sexual exploitation, bullying, crime and anti-social behaviour;
- enjoy and achieve – to be ready for and attend school, to achieve personally, socially and academically;
- make a positive contribution – play a part in decision making, developing positive relationships and self-confidence, and learning to deal with changes;
- achieve economic well-being – engage in further education or employment, live in decent homes with access to transport and material goods.

One of the main reasons for the government initiating the ECM agenda in the first place was to move the focus from *intervention* to *prevention* because:

> *Too often children experience difficulties at home or at school, but receive too little help too late, once problems have reached crisis point.*
>
> (HM Government, 2003, p5)

Every Child Matters also states that:

> *Some children will always require extra help because of the disadvantages they face. The key is to ensure children receive services at the first onset of problems, and to prevent any children slipping through the net.*
>
> (p8)

My experience as a school counsellor has shown that decisions and choices driven by personal conviction are more likely to be translated into action and this is where the role of the counsellor really comes into its own, enabling the school community to fulfil these objectives. At the same time, many more schools now employ Family Support Workers, Parent Support Advisers or even nurses and other staff in purely pastoral roles. In some schools the Head of Year is not necessarily a member of the teaching staff but someone employed for their communication and problem-solving skills in order to deal with all matters non-academic.

SCHOOL COUNSELLING: A GENERAL OVERVIEW

The employment of counsellors in schools as permanent members of staff is still a relatively new innovation. Working at a large (1,500 pupils) high school in Norfolk, I am in the privileged position of being a full-time counsellor with my own room in which to work. There are other counsellors working similarly locally and nationally but this is not the norm. Some schools may employ counsellors part time, some may use agency counsellors – for instance, through Connexions, the national youth service. Other individuals such as drug and alcohol workers may also work in schools using counselling skills.

As a school counsellor it is important to differentiate between the role of a youth worker and that of a counsellor, especially if you are considering an onward referral. It would clearly be inappropriate to have two counsellors working with one student but it might be entirely appropriate to have a youth worker and a counsellor working together. For example, a drugs worker may be able to offer expertise to help a young person address a drug problem and the counsellor may be able to work more closely with the underlying issues. It is also possible for the counsellor to work with the Child and Adolescent Mental Health Service (CAMHS, a tier 3 service) in a counselling role, as long as you liaise with them and have client consent.

However, the CAMHS team will have limited availability and are unlikely to be instantly available except in extreme circumstances.

When working with young people there are four recognised tiers of service for onward referral:

Tier 1   primary or direct contact services;
Tier 2   interventions by individuals who have specialist knowledge;
Tier 3   interventions offered by teams of specialist CAMHS staff;
Tier 4   residential specialist services.

REFLECTION POINT

What might influence your decision to refer on to another agency or even a higher tier of service? What factors would dictate your continued involvement in the case, either with the individual client or with the other service?

ACCOUNTABILITY

As a counsellor you will be a member of a relevant professional body such as BACP and therefore subscribe to their ethical guidelines. You will also be accountable to the head teacher and the governors and will need to ensure a collaborative professional relationship with them. While you will have a duty of care to the students, it is the head teacher who has the ultimate responsibility for the pupils in her school. She needs to feel assured that her counsellor, employed to support the emotional well-being of her students, is working within the school's agenda as well as to her own professional agenda. In view of recent changes within schools, which will be explored further in this chapter, there is no reason why there should be conflict between the counsellor's role and the school's agenda.

THE BASICS: SETTING UP A SCHOOLS-BASED SERVICE

Physical practicalities

Anyone who has ever worked in a school will know that space is always at a premium. As teacher roles expand and the demand for increasing evidence, tracking and the like creates ever more paperwork, teachers need office space and this inevitably squeezes the potential for the counsellor's own space.

It is the relatively few full-time school-based counsellors who are the most likely to have their own space. Over the years, I have acquired many aids to my practice and would be lost without a room to store and display them in. Not only that, counselling is a distinct relationship within a school and it is important that this is reflected in the counselling room. It should also be adolescent friendly. I have provided throws for the chairs and bright red cushions with silky spiky red 'noodles'. The young people love them and it helps them relax into the room and the counselling relationship.

ACTIVITY 1.1

With room space in schools restricted, what steps might you take as a school counsellor to ensure that, even when allocated to random classrooms, you can establish a therapeutic atmosphere with your client which will indicate to them that this is a distinctly different relationship?

CONFIDENTIALITY

The first requirement, fundamental to all counselling, is that confidentiality can be assured for the young person and the school will need to set in place such a policy before any counselling takes place.

Working with young people under 18 means there will necessarily also be issues around child protection to consider. Schools will have Child Protection policies in place and a school counsellor should make themselves familiar with the contents of these as a matter of priority. These policies will inform the counsellor as to who the designated teacher is for Child Protection. There will likely be more than one. These policies will also refer briefly to the four main categories of abuse, which are:

- physical;
- emotional;
- sexual;
- neglect.

The policy will also indicate the course of action the counsellor should take if a disclosure of a child protection nature is made. It is, sadly, inevitable that the counsellor will become extremely familiar with this process. An important factor to note here is that the counsellor does not act on the disclosure itself, but simply reports the detail of the disclosure to the designated officer, thus ensuring no clouding of the role. The counsellor should also ensure that the client is informed that information is being passed on.

Confidentiality will need to be broken if children are deemed to be either 'at risk of' or suffering 'significant harm':

There are no absolute criteria on which to rely when judging what constitutes significant harm. Consideration of the severity of ill-treatment may include the degree and the extent of physical harm, the duration and frequency of abuse and neglect, the extent of premeditation, and the presence or degree of threat, coercion, sadism and bizarre or unusual elements . . . Sometimes a single traumatic event may constitute significant harm, e.g. a violent assault, suffocation or poisoning. More often, significant harm is a compilation of significant events, both acute and long-standing, which interrupt, change or damage the child's physical and psychological development.

(Norfolk Local Safeguarding Children's Board, 2008, p30)

Confidentiality and parental consent

It is always preferable to gain parental consent when counselling those under 16 and to encourage positive communication with parents so that difficult home situations can be worked with collaboratively. However, parental anxiety can occasionally cause the parent to influence, control or manipulate the therapeutic relationship, thereby interrupting the young person's process and growth. These guidelines should be followed:

As a general principle it is legal and acceptable for a young person to ask for confidential counselling without parental consent providing they are of sufficient understanding and intelligence.

(*Gillick v West Norfolk Area Health Authority* [1985], HL, quoted in BACP, 2001, p13)

As a result of this ruling, guidelines were laid down by Lord Fraser and became known as 'Fraser guidelines', relating specifically to Gillick competent young people receiving confidential contraceptive advice. These guidelines have often been translated by other professionals as a benchmark to measure whether young people should receive other confidential services without parental consent.

In 2003, the Sexual Offences Act went still further and made it possible for non-health professional staff to give advice relating to sexual matters within certain guidelines.

It is worth researching these issues and exploring your own position regarding parental involvement. This will not be an exact science and each case will need treating individually. Young people can be quite reticent about letting parents know they are coming to counselling in the first instance. Sometimes, it is more to do with wanting their own time and space, with someone giving them full attention, and knowing that this will not be interfered with. It is about the client wanting to be in control rather than about any negative input anticipated from parents. It is often the case that once students settle into the counselling relationship, and trust grows, they themselves tell their parents in their own time.

Disclosure: who needs to know?

In cases where the child is deemed by the counsellor to be at risk:

- the counsellor will inform the client that their disclosure will need reporting to the Child Protection Officer; this should be done at the earliest opportunity and followed up in writing. Each school will have its own reporting arrangements for such instances and it is vital that the school counsellor is clear from the outset what these are;
- the counsellor should also reassure the client that their needs are paramount and that they will be supported and informed as the process develops.

In cases where the child is deemed by the counsellor *not* to be at risk:

- the counsellor will encourage the child to speak with their parents;
- the counsellor may also encourage discussion with other adults, for example teachers, where this might be helpful;
- information to others will, therefore, only be disclosed on a need-to-know basis.

The following case studies present the same problem but one is gauged as being 'not at risk' and the other has the potential to be considered 'at risk'.

Case study 1.1   Client 'not at risk'

Jemima, who is 14 years old, discloses that following a row with her mum over boyfriend issues she retreated, completely frustrated, to her room and cut her arms with a pair of scissors. The bleeding was light, though the shock to herself that she had resorted to such measures was great. The cuts were on her forearm. She had found it difficult to talk with her mum as she felt unheard and, whenever the subject was raised, an argument quickly ensued. We explored distraction techniques to cope with her desire to self-injure and she identified one or two that might work for her. She was keen to return the following week to talk further about her relationship with her boyfriend and mum in more detail. She found the distraction techniques successful and began tentatively to talk with her mum. While she self-injured on two further occasions, she subsequently stopped as her relationship with her mum improved.

Case study 1.2   Client 'at risk'

Adam, who is 15 years old, discloses that following a break-up with his girlfriend he cut one of his arms quite deeply and had continued the practice over the past fortnight on a significant number of occasions. His arms have a number of deep scratches on them and feel uncomfortable. He is also taking paracetamol as pain relief. He acts impulsively, appears depressed and is distressed throughout the session; he is not sleeping and has not told anyone else about his problem.

I gently inform him that I will need to pass this on to the designated Child Protection Officer but reassure him that, if he wishes, we can continue to spend time and look behind the self-injury and into the emotional triggers causing him to react in this way. As a result of the disclosure to the Child Protection Officer, his parents took him to his GP where a referral was made to the CAMHS team who subsequently worked with the whole family.

REFLECTION POINT

- What might be your benchmark when determining whether a client is at risk?
- What might your personal boundaries and considerations be in deciding what action to take?

In recent years, self-injury has become a major issue faced by school counsellors. It is important that school counsellors research this issue for themselves; there is much excellent material available and counsellors should also ensure access to adequate training.

I have found it useful to prepare and ask clients to complete a small questionnaire covering the basics of the self-injury. The questions consider motivation for change, strength of the urge to self-injure and success in controlling it, whether there are any suicidal thoughts and particular triggers towards self-injury. Using the brief answers on this sheet is a valuable tool when considering whether a client is 'at risk' or not. I might ask the client for permission to share this information only with the Child Protection Officer when unsure about it being a child protection issue. As I am not sharing their personal story, and only passing on the practicalities of their self-injury, clients are usually willing to allow this. Self-injury is generally a coping mechanism; the real work on the underlying issues will be processed, confidentially, in the counselling room.

SAFEGUARDING

This has become quite a buzzword in schools recently and the government has defined it as follows.

- *Protecting children and young people from maltreatment.*
- *Preventing impairment of children and young people's health and development.*
- *Ensuring that children and young people are growing up in circumstances consistent with the provision of safe and effective care.*
- *Undertaking that role as to enable those children and young people to have optimum life chances and to enter adulthood successfully.*

(HM Government, 2006, pp34–5)

In Norfolk, the Local Safeguarding Children's Board (LSCB) exists as a result of the Children Act 2004 requiring each local authority to establish such a Board. This Board is the main statutory body for agreeing how each local area will work together to safeguard and promote the welfare of children living in each authority's areas. It is also responsible for ensuring the effectiveness of agencies working within the authority.

Schools necessarily have many policies in place to support safeguarding issues. A school counsellor should make themselves familiar with the particular criteria at their school.

ACTIVITY 1.2

Using the internet, source generic school policy statements, for instance those on self-harm, anti-bullying, bereavement and loss, and child protection. As a school counsellor, which statements do you think might be essential to support your role? If the school you work in does not have such policies in place, would you feel it necessary to raise this and get certain statements agreed as policy?

CONTRACTING

Many young people will not have seen a counsellor before and will be very unsure about how the relationship might work. A contract is a useful way of informing the student about the nature of the relationship. This might seem a formal procedure and it is worth endeavouring to handle it as informally as possible, without minimising its importance. The contract I use is based loosely on BACP guidelines.

Sample contract

I, ... understand and agree that:

- The counsellor will not provide solutions for me but will try to help me find my own solutions.
- What I say will be in confidence unless I say something that indicates serious risk to me, or to anyone else, in which case the counsellor will discuss what she will say and to whom she will speak.
- Coming to counselling is my choice and I have a choice about what I do or don't do, within the counselling process. [*I explain here that sometimes I might work creatively but they are under no obligation to do so should I suggest such an activity.*]
- One session may be all I need but if I wish to continue coming for further sessions I can discuss this and make further appointments.
- If I fail to turn up for an appointment the counsellor will send me a note. If I do not respond to this within a week and later decide I want an appointment, I understand that I may have to wait for another appointment and that my name may be added to a waiting list.

Signed .... Date..

It is also important to stress to the young person that while the counsellor is the adult in the room and will oversee the session, the relationship will aim to be one of equality. Person-centred therapy in particular maintains that clients are the experts on their own lives. The counsellor is there to support and facilitate change; the client is in the driving seat. This is an extremely important statement to make with regard to a school setting as young people are often so conditioned to being directed by adults who wish to control, who 'know best' or who may even manipulate them. The offer of a relationship fundamentally different from the norm is usually perceived as a refreshing and welcome change.

ACTIVITY 1.3

Schools are unlikely to have in place policies to cover every eventuality. For example, there may be no individual policy on self-injury, or eating disorders.

- How will you gauge whether you are dealing with a child 'at risk'?
- Where could you get advice?
- Bearing in mind the contract you have signed with your client, to whom could you talk in such instances?

THE COMMON ASSESSMENT FRAMEWORK

Recent legislation under the ECM agenda has also introduced the CAF to practitioners working with children and young people.

The CAF is a key part of delivering frontline services that are integrated, and are focused around the needs of children and young people. The CAF is a standardised approach to conducting assessments of children's additional needs and deciding how these should be met. It can be used by practitioners across children's services in England.

The CAF promotes more effective, earlier identification of additional needs, particularly in universal services. It aims to provide a simple process for a holistic assessment of children's needs and strengths; taking account of the roles of parents, carers and environmental factors on their development. Practitioners are then better placed to agree with children and families about appropriate modes of support. The CAF also aims to improve integrated working by promoting coordinated service provisions.

(Department for Children, Schools and Families,
**www.dcsf.gov.uk/everychildmatters/strategy/
deliveringservices1/caf/cafframework/**)

School counsellors will regularly have occasion to refer on to other organisations or agencies. It is now necessary to use the CAF process in order to access other agency support. This will involve a potentially detailed form to complete with your client, although completing minimal details is generally acceptable and may be more conducive to working with the child as the forwarding agency will inevitably have their own paperwork to complete. CAF training is available locally and all paperwork available on the government *Every Child Matters* website (see URL above).

Case study 1.3

A young Year 8 male self-referred for counselling. He was concerned about the issue of confidentiality. I had heard that smoking might be an issue for him. He confirmed this. I felt a referral to a drugs agency would best meet his needs. I completed the CAF form, which the agency then picked up. While they worked confidentially with him, the CAF was logged centrally so that should other agencies become involved at a later date they had knowledge of this initial referral.

RESTORATIVE APPROACHES AS APPLIED IN A SCHOOL SETTING

Over recent years the government has been keen to encourage the implementation of a restorative agenda in many settings, most noticeably perhaps, in the criminal justice system. This is being rolled out to other departments and is filtering into the school system. Restorative approaches are, broadly, a way of working restoratively in relationships where there has been harm to one or more individuals, or where there is conflict.

The Restorative Justice Council defines it thus:

> *Restorative Justice works to resolve conflict and repair harm. It encourages those who have caused harm to acknowledge the impact of what they have done and gives them an opportunity to make reparation. It offers those who have suffered harm the opportunity to have their harm or loss acknowledged and amends made.*
>
> *Conflict between people is inevitable, but when it occurs restorative justice can help to restore the balance in a just and fair way. In resolving the harm done it works to prevent it happening again.*
>
> **(www.restorativejustice.org.uk/?What_is_Restorative_Justice%3F** downloadable leaflet 'What is RJ?')

It might also be best understood by comparing it with retributive or traditional justice, which asks, in cases of conflict: 'What school rule has been broken?'; 'Who is to blame?'; 'What punishment is appropriate?'; Whereas, by contrast, restorative justice asks: 'Who has been hurt?'; 'What are their needs?'; 'Whose responsibility are they?'.

Applied as a whole school ethos, this has the potential to dramatically impact on a school's success and well-being, and the school counsellor is well placed and qualified to implement such initiatives. Further training is necessary and an internet search will highlight accredited trainers in your area. The Restorative Justice Council is at the heart of this initiative and provides advice and guidance across the board. In a school where concentrated numbers of students are learning to make relationships, working restoratively when things go wrong is an extremely powerful way of repairing the damage. There are a number of guidelines to working restoratively but the main ones are that:

- the primary aim should be the repair of harm;
- there should be agreement about essential facts of the incident and an acceptance of some involvement by the person who caused the harm;
- participation should be voluntary for all participants and based on informed choice;
- there should be respect for the feelings of all participants.

Restorative practitioners must be seen as neutral by participants, and act impartially.

Burnside and Baker (1994, p109) note that

> *Evidence from the USA suggests that a dollar invested in preventative work with children and families will in time save seven dollars which would otherwise have been spent on various forms of adult incarceration and the associated costs of the criminal justice process.*

I was recently able to present a case, with the backing of senior leadership, to work restoratively with students in cases of conflict. Two of the middle managers immediately gave me a number of referrals and this work has been some of the most successful and powerful I have done in school. The young people responded positively to working restoratively as neither party felt threatened and both felt heard.

THE UNIQUENESS OF THE SETTING

Whatever their counselling orientation, the school counsellor will need to be creative in their work with young people. I seriously doubt it is possible, for instance, to work as a classic person-centred counsellor in a high school setting. Bear in mind that you will be working with pupils aged between 11 and 16, or 18 if the school has a sixth form. It is true that some students may well be emotionally mature enough to work with a counsellor in much the same way as an adult would, but many will not. It is the counsellor's responsibility to make the service accessible.

It is possible to do this in any number of ways. It would be helpful to complete additional training geared around working with young people. This might include topics such as neuro-linguistic programming, the use of role play or restorative justice training, or by simply using some creative activities as detailed below. There are many courses available to schools and it is extremely likely that relevant literature will arrive on your desk advertising such courses. Choose wisely, however, for money is always stretched in education and you will be limited as to the courses you will be able to attend, so ensure that you can justify their value to your work.

WORKING CREATIVELY

Miniature animals

An effective creative activity is the use of miniature animals, such as children's farm animals or zoo animals, to tell a client's story (Gelard and Gelard, 2009). The counsellor asks the client to choose an animal from a varied selection to represent themselves and then different animals to represent other people, perhaps those with whom they're having difficulties or those they are particularly close to. The counsellor then asks the client to place the animals in a tableau where they would be comfortable. She might also ask them to move one animal close to another. The beauty of this is that it enables the client to talk about the animals while actually talking about their situation, which in some ways distances them from it and makes exploration safer.

Case study 1.4   Sarah

Sarah was struggling with relationships at home. Her parents, who lived separately with new partners, were rowing, both on the phone and when Sarah was dropped off to one or the other. She felt stuck in the middle of their arguments and was questioned by both parents about the other's life. Sarah was an only child and a younger member of the school. She found it difficult to expand very much on her situation. I used the miniature animals with her and asked her to select a figure to represent herself. She chose a rat. This immediately opened up the therapeutic dialogue and gave me a clear indication of how she was feeling in her family setting. She chose strong, powerful animals to represent her parents. This imagery was able to move the counselling relationship on enormously and really helped Sarah talk out how she felt, understand the dynamics of her situation and explore what she might be able to do to change things.

The 'Tree Test'

Another example of working creatively is taken from the 'Tree Test' or 'Baum Test' developed by Koch (1952) as a diagnostic tool to work with children. Again, for those clients who are struggling to articulate their feelings but are happy to be creative and draw, I adapt this test by asking the young client to draw themselves as a tree, to include others in their social circle and position and draw them similarly. It is important for the counsellor to remain present though not intrusive with the client while they draw and not to question at this stage. However, once the drawing is complete, much discussion can be generated by exploring the picture together. As with the miniature animals, it draws out a client's story and gives a vehicle for understanding, re-framing and movement. However, guard against using this to interpret or diagnose, mainly because it might introduce new material completely beyond the client's perspective and unrelated to the work currently being undertaken.

My therapy room is papered with such pictures. I have sought the permission of the artists to display their work and speak anonymously about their stories. Each one is very different, telling an equally powerful and individual story.

Emotions characters

Another way of working creatively is to use pictures of cartoon-style characters expressing various emotions set in a single picture. The client simply colours in any of the figures they feel represent their current state and this provides opportunity for exploration. This can also be helpful as an evaluation tool if it is used at the beginning of the counselling sessions and again at the end. The two pictures can be compared to see how the client's perceptions have changed through the counselling process.

It is my belief that integration in school counselling is preferable to eclecticism. Worsley defines integration as, *What is integrated is any knowledge that helps me understand the client, her process, myself and the therapy* (Worsley, 2007, p11). Eclecticism, meaning, 'I select', suggests a random selection of techniques with little thought to fundamental beliefs around values and theory.

ROUTES INTO SCHOOL COUNSELLING

Currently, a diploma in counselling is generally considered sufficient for entry into school counselling but most schools are likely to require some additional evidence that a counsellor can work successfully with young people. This might include experience of having worked in other agencies with young people, or having had another role within a school.

It is not necessary to have specific training with young people unless you plan to work with children under the age of 11, in which case a diploma in play therapy would be an appropriate route in. You will need to demonstrate the ability to work as part of a team while maintaining client confidentiality. Jobs for school counsellors are still very few and far between and competition for posts is fierce.

One way of moving into the school environment is to approach schools as a volunteer counsellor in the first instance. To do this, you will need a clear understanding of how your service will integrate into the school and you will need to articulate this successfully.

Research summary

BACP have recently completed some very timely research into school counselling and I would particularly like to draw on some of their findings which resonate with my own experience.

Clearly, the role of counsellor and that of teacher are very different. Counsellors operate from a position of equality with their client and may well be non-directive; teachers hold power and are very clearly directive in their approach. Relationships with key staff are, therefore, very important. Indeed, the influence of school leadership was highlighted in the research:

> References to power relationships infused participants' accounts. Some participants came into direct conflict with school leadership over their management style, and particularly challenging incidents involved some element of shaming. . . Whilst counsellors were able to compensate for institutional insensitivity, this was not without personal consequences. All four counsellors engaged independently or via an agency decided to leave their schools, and two of these did so in response to feeling abused or witnessing abuse or neglect perpetrated by leaders in school.
>
> (Harris, 2009, p178)

This seems a rather bleak picture but it is worth noting that the counsellors engaged in the research mentioned here were part-time. It would be difficult for them, perhaps, to have much influence in their school and to have the opportunity to build relationships with senior leaders.

The research concludes:

> The findings from this study indicate that as counsellors are introduced into schools, the quality of communication that takes place between them and senior staff has a direct impact upon establishment of their services. Equally, the availability of counsellors to be aware of and communicate with other staff seems to have a positive influence on the referral processes to and from counsellors. Although counsellors are able to find ways of working alongside other services and agencies, more could be done to ensure these processes satisfy the demands of counselling in school services, for example referral systems and processes, and access to multi-agency resources. Given the current strategic directives in increasing the delivery of counselling in school across the UK it is an important time to carefully consider how to best provide efficient and effective services.
>
> (ibid., p185)

> We are all aware that counselling is about the relationship – the relationship with the client. It is, however, the wise school counsellor who gives time and energy in making it about building positive relationships with teachers and senior leadership. While you will not win everyone over, you can influence many and this will, without doubt, determine to a large extent the success of your practice in a school setting.

CONCLUSION

While I have explored new pastoral initiatives within the wider role of schools, the truth is that schools remain institutions whose success is measured against academic achievement. Thorne (2008) takes a particular view:

> *The insistent language of standard raising permeates not only our educational system but, progressively, every area of our national life. Standards we are told, must be 'driven up', 'ratcheted up', 'forced up' . . . It is a language of coercion and obsessionality, which induces fear and guilt while claiming to be a language of encouragement dedicated to creating a more equal society and giving the public the services it deserves. League tables proliferate, naming and shaming are a public sport and for the successful there is the allurement of financial reward and accelerated promotion . . . This performance-surveillance culture is, it is claimed, necessary for the cultivation of a work-force which will ensure economic prosperity for the future. This unquestioned assumption has, as far as I know, never been empirically tested despite the fact that there are countries whose economic success does not seem to correlate at all convincingly with the mean level of educational attainment of its population. Even if it were true, however, it would scarcely be sufficient reason for the creation of a generation which shows every sign of rampant psychological disorder.*

> (p42)

The objectives of the school counsellor are not rooted in educational success but in emotional health, and clearly there is a correlation: students achieve more when they are psychologically and emotionally well, but the primary driver of decision making in schools will likely always be academic success. I am privileged to work in a school that actively seeks to support the emotional health of its students. My work has impacted on lives way beyond the attainment of GCSEs and the like. As I write, I am preparing to support a young client in court over sexual abuse that occurred many years ago. I have spent many hours in the counselling room with this client, experienced 'relational depth' and shared her tears. She is testament to the benefits of counselling in a school setting; she is strong yet vulnerable and has an emotional maturity way beyond her years, partly facilitated by the sharing of her journey with her counsellor. She will make a success of her life, not solely because she is bright and will achieve academically but primarily because she is emotionally mature and throughout the counselling relationship has dared to go places she might have struggled to access alone. While it has been a difficult and costly journey for us both, it has been my privilege to walk it with her and I would certainly neither trade the experience nor the relationship.

CHAPTER SUMMARY

Counselling is generally perceived as a fairly solitary occupation. If employed in a school setting, you will likely be the sole counsellor on the staff. While you might be part of a pastoral team, your role, and the boundaries of confidentiality within which counsellors work, may leave you feeling quite isolated while teachers and others are able to discuss students openly. Balanced with this are the requirements of policies such as Safe-guarding, *Every Child Matters* and the Common Assessment Framework, to name but a few. These initiatives may require you to engage and potentially share information. You will need to consider this carefully, being mindful that the relationship with your client remains confidential. These competing requirements are not easy to navigate and need consideration, and the support of a suitably qualified supervisor. It is helpful if you can find a supervisor who has experience of working with young people. Do not work without regular, clinical supervision; ensure this is in your job description and if you are a direct employee of a school you should expect that the school will pay for it. As a school counsellor, some of your major challenges and frustrations are likely to be around structures and where the role sits within the school. New counsellors would be strongly advised to set parameters in consultation with senior leaders as soon as they are in post and to work closely with their supervisor to ensure ongoing collaborative relationships within the school.

Inevitably, the young people themselves present their own idiosyncrasies. They are neither young children nor fully formed adults and are at a devel-opmental stage that needs to be understood and worked with. Counsellors of adolescents need to be in touch with their own inner adolescent. Although settling into the role of school counsellor presents certain challenges, it nevertheless provides opportunity for some of the most inspirational and exciting work one could hope to achieve in the coun-selling arena.

SUGGESTED FURTHER READING

Bor, R (2002) *Counselling in Schools*. London: Sage.

An in-depth, straightforward and practical guide to school counselling.

Gelard, K and Gelard, D (2009) *Counselling Adolescents*, 3rd edition. London: Sage.

A popular introduction to the specific issues associated with counselling adolescents; a clear and useful guide for school counsellors.

Hopkins, B (2004) *A Whole School Approach to Restorative Justice*. London: Jessica Kingsley Publishers.

A step-by-step guide to introducing restorative approaches in schools; very straightforward and thorough.

Sunderland, M (2008) *Draw on Your Emotions*. Milton Keynes: Speechmark Publishing.

Practical ways of working with children and young people in a creative manner.

Thorne, B (2008) *Infinitely Beloved*. London: Darton, Longman and Todd.

An exploration of theological and psychological contributions to understanding the human person.

Thorsborne, M and Vinegrad, D (2009) *Restorative Justice Pocketbook*. Hampshire: Teacher's Pocketbooks.

A cartoon-style, practical guide to the working of restorative approaches in a school setting.

Worsley, R (2007) *The Integrative Counselling Primer*. Herefordshire: PCCS Books.

A succinct guide to integrative theory and practice for everyone wanting an authoritative synopsis.

CHAPTER 2

Counselling in Further Education (FE) colleges

Cathy Austin

CORE KNOWLEDGE

- College counsellors have to be robust and flexible, able to speak the language of management as well as understand and speak the language of their students.
- Many students find themselves in a hostile world, their families may have disintegrated, they feel no one takes a real interest in them; they often have difficulties maintaining relationships themselves.
- Clients in FE often present with complex and difficult problems. Counsellors need to be familiar with local specialist agencies and their referral procedures.

INTRODUCTION

In this chapter we will consider the history of counselling in the FE sector and explore how the job evolved from a 'Jack-of-all-trades' to a professional clinical role firmly embedded in the structure of the institution. The chapter will look at the changes in the student population from the 1970s to today and at the impact these changes have had on our work. We will consider the main presenting issues for today's students and assess the present situation in FE colleges. The main challenges facing today's FE counsellors include:

- fears for the future due to financial constraints and changing management attitudes;
- how to manage ever-increasing workloads in the light of these constraints and attitude changes;
- the challenges of working with some very troubled young people (16–19-year-olds) in an educational setting.

Many FE counsellors work increasingly in isolation. The chapter will also explore, therefore, the networks that exist nationally to offer help and support to counsellors working in colleges. It will also look at local agencies and professional organisations that exist to help our students if, as counsellors, we are unable to do so.

Finally, I would like to remind myself, and those counsellors coming after me, why this is perhaps the most challenging but potentially the most rewarding of all counselling work.

THE HISTORY OF COUNSELLING IN FE COLLEGES

Further Education in the 1970s

FE colleges evolved out of the technical colleges. They traditionally attracted students who were more practically minded than academic. These students studied carpentry and catering and did apprenticeships. FE colleges also attracted students who were fed up with the constraints of school and wanted a more adult environment in which to study A levels and GCSEs with the idea of going on to university. College is very different from school; students need to be self-motivated and self-disciplined.

In the 1970s student counsellors were expected to fulfil a number of roles. Kirby (1974, quoted in Bell 1996, p18), writing about the counselling service in North Nottinghamshire College of FE, identified four functions of a counsellor:

1. educational guidance;
2. vocational guidance;
3. personal counselling;
4. liaison with allied services.

A typical team in the 1970s consisted of a Head and Deputy Head of Student Services, an international student adviser and a student counsellor. The staff would normally have backgrounds in teaching, careers and social work as there was little or no professional counselling training available at this time.

A medical centre might also have been part of Student Services and the Student Union, although independent, would also usually have been linked to Student Services as well. It wasn't uncommon for there to be several receptionists who fielded calls, answered questions, made appointments and even cups of tea for students waiting to see a counsellor or a nurse. These services were often centrally located with a large seating area where students could just chill out.

The 1980s and 1990s: changing attitudes to counselling in FE

In the 1980s and 1990s counselling emerged as an important part of the support system for students and this was a time for the development of the role of counselling services, a process that was often supported by colleagues in college management.

Case study 2.1   Example of the development of a service

Initially I was shocked at the levels of misery, lack of parental support and general isolation so many of our students seemed to be experiencing and I wanted to take them all home! It soon became apparent to me that there were many students who needed more time because of problems they were encountering either at college or at home. These students could not be sent elsewhere or quickly stitched up and sent on their way.

It was then that I also realised that I was not qualified to tackle the complexity of the issues I had to deal with every day. I came from a background in social work, working primarily with young people and families, and had completed a one-year advanced training in Transactional Analysis but had had no formal counselling training.

My Head of Student Services and the college management could not have been more supportive. The college paid for me to do a three-year part-time postgraduate Counselling Diploma, paid for my supervision and accreditation and gradually the job became manageable. We took on more staff, a part-time financial adviser, and an admin assistant so all students' needs were dealt with in one place quickly and efficiently.

In the 1980s and 1990s counselling rapidly developed as a profession and became very much embedded in the structure of most FE colleges. Counsellors sat on staff/student committees, ran workshops on such topics as working with difficult students, when to refer to a counsellor and the role of the tutor. They were involved in writing policies on child protection, working with suicidal students, and confidentiality and data protection.

At this time an increasing number of mature students began to enter FE colleges. Some had worked for several years, some had been made redundant and some had been unemployed for many years. Access funds enabled many young mums and dads to return to study and embark upon Access courses that were equivalent to A levels. These courses were designed to fit in with school hours and were very popular. In the mid-1990s over half of the FE students in the author's college were over 25. Postgraduate and Degree courses were also set up, offering an alternative to traditional

HE provision and blurring the boundaries somewhat between Further and Higher Education.

Despite the growth in student numbers, the student to counsellor ratio remained low in FE (in the author's experience, one qualified counsellor to 20,000 students). The majority of students were part-time but still had access to the counselling service. Requests for more counselling staff were often, and continue to be, met with arguments about lack of money and accommodation.

The comparisons with counselling provision in the local Higher Education (HE) institution at this time would provoke feelings of envy, given the difficulties faced by FE counsellors. HE counselling services often had a team of counsellors working from a dedicated building with their own reception staff. Compared with our university colleagues, FE counsellors have often felt like the poor relation, particularly in terms of salaries and facilities. At the same time, working mostly with 16–19-year-olds can be particularly challenging. The young students' often chaotic lifestyles, the constant pushing of boundaries and their tangible need for a good solid parent figure often stretches the FE counsellor's resources to the limit.

SUPPORT FOR FE COUNSELLORS

The Association for Student Counselling (ASC) was set up in 1970 and as the AUCC (Association for University and College Counsellors) it continues to provide a very much needed forum of support and professional guidance today. In 1986 at the AGM of the ASC it was agreed to organise an FE sub-committee in recognition of the particular needs of those of us working in this area.

The email **counsellors-in-fe@jiscmail.ac.uk** is probably one of the best forms of support and information for FE counsellors there is. It is a place where all counsellors in FE in the UK can talk to each other via email about anything at all. Debates over the last year include applying for accreditation, what we can offer when a student dies, waiting lists, providing workshops on exam stress and the threats to our service.

The AUCC currently provides an annual conference with speakers, workshops and networking opportunities. It also produces a journal and has an advisory service.

REFLECTION POINT

- Has your experience and training prepared you for working with 16–19-year-olds?
- Has your experience and training prepared you for working with mature students within an educational context?
- What additional training needs might you have?

COUNSELLING IN FE TODAY: FURTHER CHANGES IN THE STUDENT POPULATION

Today, mature student numbers have declined as there are fewer courses that cater for their needs and there is less financial help available. International student numbers have also declined due to high fees and visa restrictions.

In recent years there has been a massive increase in young students who have not previously had good experiences in education attending FE colleges. In 1999, the acronym NEETs was coined by New Labour's Geoff Mulgan to describe people 'Not in Education, Employment or Training'. Government policy has been to target these groups, to get them off benefits and into the workforce. Apprenticeships have come back onto the FE menu and, sponsored by government funds, they have proved to be very popular with students.

Educational Maintenance Allowances or EMAs were introduced by the government in 2004 and have made a big difference to the numbers of young students attending FE colleges. EMAs were brought in to reduce the numbers of 16-year-olds dropping out from education and they enable students between the ages of 16 and 19 to claim between £10 and £30 per week for attending certain college courses. The allowance is conditional on attendance and is means tested. Students get a £100 bonus for every six months they stay in education.

Many of the students receiving EMAs would otherwise have left education at the school leaving age; many have learning difficulties and some have quite complex mental health problems. Anecdotally, it appears that FE counsellors increasingly see a lot of students diagnosed with autism and Attention Deficit Hyperactivity Disorder (ADHD).

There is also a Learner Support Fund available to all students, which, since April 2010, comes via the local authorities for the under 19s and via the

Skills Funding Agency for students aged 19 and over, and is held and managed by the colleges. This includes funding for childcare and in addition there are central government schemes for childcare.

Increasing access to education is a laudable aim but the funds to give students the extra emotional support they so often need are either not forthcoming or woefully inadequate. This lack of resources inevitably impacts on counselling services as teaching staff refer more students for counselling because they do not know how to handle behaviours sometimes associated with specific learning disabilities.

RISK MANAGEMENT AND APPROPRIATE REFERRALS

An important role of a counselling service in FE is to provide guidance to the institution regarding working with students in distress or with mental health and emotional needs.

Some students are not able to cope with the pressures of college life. They may need a place of safety – a hospital and a prison cell are both considered safe places. Students who are at risk often live on the edge, neglecting themselves, sometimes endangering their lives or putting others at risk. They may have had chaotic and damaging early life experiences and it is likely that some of these students can be helped by counselling. However, others cannot, and counsellors in FE often need to remind staff that counselling is not a disciplinary procedure; it only works if a student wants to come. Counsellors need to maintain certain boundaries and cannot be expected to:

- go to the aid of a student who is drunk or suspected of being on drugs;
- placate a student who is extremely angry or upset.

Guidance to staff confronted by behaviour which may be the result of a serious emotional disorder and where they fear the behaviour may result in threat or damage to self or others is clear and unequivocal. Staff must either call site services or call the police.

The college and its staff (including the counselling service) need to have a clear understanding of their boundaries and limitations.

REFLECTION POINT

The role of counsellors in FE colleges is often misunderstood by management and academic staff. In terms of your counselling experience so far, consider the following questions.

- What are the best ways to inform colleagues about where our roles begin and end?
- Can counselling ever appropriately be seen as an emergency service?
- Can students with mental health difficulties be helped by counselling?
- Are there students who cannot be helped by counselling? If so, what action would you take to ensure they receive the appropriate care?

CHANGING ATTITUDES AND THE SHIFTING TERMINOLOGY OF STUDENT SUPPORT

The last five years have seen dramatic changes, not only in the student population but also in attitudes towards student support. Financial constraints, with an emphasis on retention rates, have set the scene for sweeping changes in the structure of FE colleges.

At the beginning of the new century, money was made available to update and redesign old and outdated buildings. A twenty-first century, world-class college was considered to need a centralised administration, open-plan offices and to be student-centred and business-like. Terminology was changed as 'students' became 'learners'; 'Student Services' changed to 'Learner Support' and then underwent a further transformation into the open-plan 'Advice Shops' that exist in some colleges today.

Although the money for the rebuilds was subsequently retracted, many FE colleges had already started on a programme of change and, as a result, many counsellors faced upheaval in their working environment.

Nationally, counselling services in FE colleges are in a state of transition. College managers have to be positive and upbeat, emphasising success rates and future goals. Words like 'well-being' and 'coaching' are creeping into the job titles of counselling staff. Counsellors are required to keep up to date with emerging and changing policies such as those regarding child protection, now under the banner of Safeguarding. (Chapter 1 offers a more detailed account of changes in this arena.)

Counselling services are usually required to provide annual statistics that show not only the numbers that come for counselling but also the positive effect of counselling on retention rates. The role of the counselling service needs not only to improve the student experience but also to enable the institution to provide a duty of care to its community.

Research summary

The following are some statistics taken from an FE Counselling Service Annual Report for 2008–9 (Norwich City College (2009) *Counselling Report 2008–9*, **www.ccn.ac.uk**).

- The counselling service supported 206 students in 777 hours of counselling.
- 72 per cent of counselling clients required only 1–3 sessions.
- 85 per cent of counselling clients were full-time FE students.
- 78.5 per cent of counselling clients were female.
- 62.2 per cent of counselling clients were 16–19-year-olds.
- 94 per cent of students who accessed the counselling service in 2008–9 continued or completed their course.
- 20 per cent of counselling clients were on medication for mental health problems.
- 66 per cent of sessions dealt with issues to do with relationships.
- 49 per cent of clients were assessed at their initial session as presenting with a severity level of '4'. (*The issue is causing considerable anxiety and distress which is in turn affecting several areas of functioning* according to the AUCC 'Categories of Concern' used in most FE and HE institutions.)

COMMON PRESENTING PROBLEMS IN FE

Some of the common themes presented in FE counselling are detailed below, with a particular emphasis on the issues arising for 16–19-year-old students.

- Problems of adjusting to freedom and responsibility in terms of both work and social life.
- For some students the sense of release from the rigidity of school life can be so freeing that they may seem to go out of control for a while.
- Wearing what they like, piercing what they like and asking the age-old questions 'Who am I?', 'Where am I going?', 'What do I want to do with my life?'
- Students may be kicked out of the family home at this time and 'sofa-surfing' can become a way of life for the young, vulnerable, but often difficult-to-live-with teenager.
- Existing tensions in step-families can increase to breaking point and young people can feel that nobody really cares about them.

- Loneliness and homesickness: this can be an insurmountable problem for some younger students forced to live away from their families.
- International students may experience cultural, physical and emotional isolation.
- Course content: some subjects such as 'Childcare' require students to reflect on their own childhood experiences, which can sometimes expose painful memories that have been pushed into the background.
- Childhood sexual, physical and emotional abuse: these are frequent issues that students bring to the counsellor, often disclosing abuse for the first time. Sometimes, students have had bad experiences of disclosing abuse at school when it has immediately become a child protection issue and they have not been allowed to process their feelings.
- Problems of self-discipline and motivation: for some students the need for exploring social life and new experiences is often stronger than the need to study.
- Drug and alcohol abuse: this is a problem that is rising among young people.
- Counsellors are also presented with problems following bad experiences with drugs or alcohol – for example, panic attacks, paranoia, inability to concentrate on their studies, rape and drug- or alcohol-induced violence.
- Problems around loss: the experience of loss may be new to a young person and loss can be associated with many circumstances, including the following:
  - break-up of a relationship;
  - miscarriage or abortion;
  - rape, sexual abuse, loss of trust, innocence and childhood;
  - death of a parent, sibling or grandparent. Often a death experienced in childhood is dealt with at a later date.
  - divorce, separation of parents, loss of security;
  - loss of confidence, due, for example, to bullying;
  - loss due to illnesses or accidents. Often students become carers for their parents and try to fit in college around their responsibilities at home;
  - leaving home, loss of security.

Older students can obviously experience all of the above, but problems specific to mature students in FE tend to revolve around juggling home, college, partners, children and study. Some mature students undergo a drastic revision of their lives and sense of identity. Returning to education can also involve financial loss and loss of status.

Case study 2.2   Example of the need for client readiness in FE counselling

Rachel was so entrenched in her way of viewing the world that no one could reach her. She was 17 and studying on a Childcare course. Her tutors were increasingly concerned for her safety as she was very depressed, and had told one of them that she was bulimic and she was cutting her arms. Her academic work was adequate and she was managing reasonably well in her placements. Her tutor suggested she come for counselling, which she did somewhat unwillingly.

She did not trust anyone; she just wanted to work with children to give them the love she never had. She could not talk about why she hated herself so much. She came for a few sessions but was not ready or able at that point to really look at the reasons for her self-destructiveness. Her attendance at college dwindled; she didn't turn up on time at her placements and was eventually asked to leave the course.

Rachel enrolled on another course the following year and came for counselling again. This time she was able to make sense of some of her earlier behaviour and passed her course successfully. Rachel is an example of how young students often dip in and out of counselling. When they are ready to work at something they will. Counsellors in FE need to be flexible to allow this to happen.

REFLECTION POINT

Working with the young students in an FE college can be very challenging. The roller-coaster nature of adolescence tends to be heightened in the college atmosphere. Peer pressure, time-limits and hormones all compete for top billing, and counselling can be picked up and forgotten about in the wink of an eye! Many of these students also yearn for strong adult figures who are on their side and who are strong enough to challenge their behaviour and suggest alternative ways of being.

Consider the nature of your own counselling training.

- If you are philosophically committed to a particular way of working, how might you need to adapt your practice for the FE environment?
- What continuing professional development (CPD) training might you need to undertake to fulfil this role?

ACTIVITY 2.1

The following are several scenarios encountered by counsellors in FE. Consider how you might work with these concerns and what other sources of help there might be in your area to which you could refer students.

- A student presents in a very depressed state because she is caring for an ill parent. She is stuck at home most of the time, unable to leave and feel as though no one cares about or supports her.
- A student wants help for his cannabis use and came to counselling because his girlfriend and parents were worried about his smoking. The student acknowledges the impact of smoking marijuana on his motivation and ability to keep up with academic work but says he enjoys smoking with his friends.
- A female student comes to counselling because her boyfriend (who is a heavy drug user) has become seriously mentally ill.
- A young male student comes for counselling after being diagnosed with Aspergers Syndrome.
- An international student presents with symptoms of trauma and panic following imprisonment and torture in his country of origin.
- A vulnerable female student comes to counselling and talks of her chaotic family life, where there are often violent rows between her parents. The student escapes her family environment by cutting her arms in secret.
- A young man presents for counselling following violent rows with his mother; he is now sleeping on his friend's sofa.
- A young man presents for counselling devastated because his relationship with his girlfriend has ended. This was his first relationship and he generally does not know how to approach the opposite sex.
- A female student presents for counselling having been raped after a night out clubbing. The police have been involved and are investigating.
- A student presents for counselling after discovering she is pregnant. She wants to talk through the options available to her.

SIGNPOSTING

- Young carers can be supported by local organisations – see **www.careforcarers.co.uk**. These agencies sometimes take young people for days out, offer them support and give them a chance to meet others in the same situation.
- Drug and alcohol agencies provide specialist counselling for young people – **www.al-anonuk.org.uk** has details of local meetings and support groups for those living with relatives with drink problems. Alateen is aimed at young people between the ages of 12 and 17.

- International students, including asylum seekers and refugees, often need trauma treatment from the counselling service. **www.redcross. org.uk** can help to provide much needed support in the form of housing, financial and legal advice. The Home Office has a special unit set up to deal with all issues surrounding arranged marriages.
- Students with eating disorders can be very challenging for the FE counsellor – **www.b-eat.co.uk** provides details of local support agencies.
- It is important for counsellors to have links with the local Mental Health Care Trust.

Case study 2.3   Example of an 'emergency'

Diana came as an emergency via her tutor. She had just found out that her mother's partner was coming out of prison. He was convicted of downloading child pornography, he was violent towards her mother and cheated on her many times. Diana cannot understand how her mother can take him back. Diana is studying for a degree and does not think she can concentrate on her studies living in the same house as this man. On the other hand, she is worried about leaving her mother with him. Diana is very upset and anxious and needed somewhere to come and talk this through in confidence and to look at her options.

Case study 2.4   Example of a 'withdrawal'

Matt came to do an Access course in Social Work but was really not well enough mentally. Drugs and drink have continued to contribute to his agitation, paranoia and mood swings while at college. He was desperate to complete the course successfully but has not been able to concentrate. His counsellor strongly suggested getting some medication from the doctor, which he did. He had to work to fund the course and was living in a bedsit. He made a real effort to give up cannabis and alcohol, often succeeding for weeks at a time, but could not keep up with the work and eventually left after the Christmas break. The counsellor saw him for eight sessions and he hopes to return to college next year.

Case study 2.5   Example of a 'success'

Simon came for help with anger management. He was doing a Foundation course and had been told that if he had any more outbursts of temper he would have to leave the college. Simon talked with his counsellor about his school life, which had been very unhappy. His parents had split up and he also had girlfriend problems. He wanted to meet new people and make friends. By the end of the year Simon had a new girlfriend, had organised two holidays and many days out for all his classmates. He had successfully held down a job placement, had stopped playing so many computer games and was visibly more happy and relaxed.

Just having some time to talk about his worries and to look at the impact he had on others was a real novelty and a turning point for Simon. He came for 18 sessions and is continuing onto another course. He will come for counselling again if he needs to.

GENERAL ISSUES FOR COUNSELLORS IN FE TO CONSIDER

Referrals

About 50 per cent of referrals come from tutors. The other 50 per cent come mainly from self-referrals, but also at the suggestion of friends, family, GPs and other agencies. Tutors who have concerns about a student may make several attempts to persuade them to access counselling support; students may get as far as emailing, phoning and making an appointment, but they may still not come through the door. It is not easy to come for counselling.

Missed appointments or 'DNAs'

Missed appointments or 'DNAs' where the client 'Did Not Attend' are a complex phenomenon and an occupational hazard common to all FE counselling services. Services sometimes make allowances for this in their appointment systems, often overbooking in anticipation of no-shows. In some colleges the DNA rate is as high as 25 per cent, as a straw poll on the counsellors-in-FE email discovered in January 2010. The following are some common reasons for missed appointments.

- Very often students simply forget that they have an appointment, which is not that surprising when many of them are living quite chaotic lives.
- A client's emotional state may have changed from when they made the appointment and either they are afraid they will have nothing to talk about, they are concerned about wasting the counsellor's time or they don't want to run the risk of being reminded about their problems.
- It is difficult to come for counselling, especially if you are fearful of what may come up. Students may make and miss several appointments before they find the courage to attend.

- The initial appointments may have been made following pressure from another source, e.g. a tutor, and the student is not motivated to attend.
- Sometimes a counselling appointment is quite inappropriate and not what the student was looking for at all.
- A large number of counselling appointments are rearranged due to illness, exams or pressure of work, or class clashes due to changes of timetables.

Unattended appointments do not represent wasted hours. As noted above, some services overbook and do not keep a waiting list as they rely on the level of DNAs to keep the workload manageable. Most counsellors aim to see a maximum of five clients in a day but it is not unusual to have six students booked in each day with the expectation that one or two will not attend.

If services have the capacity, a phone call or text to the student either the day before or on the morning of their first appointment to remind them to attend can reduce the number of DNAs.

Very often when there is a cancellation, counsellors have to take the opportunity to fit in tutors, other students or emergency appointments. This is also valuable time to catch up with other work such as emails, statistics, telephone calls, research, report writing and liaising with other staff.

Male clients in FE

It is well known nationally that males are less likely to access any kind of emotional or medical support than females. However, the statistics about completed suicides, physical health and academic achievement indicate that this is not always a successful strategy. Three times as many men as women kill themselves according to figures released by the Office for National Statistics (Office for National Statistics, 2010, p2).

Case study 2.6   Example of long-term work with a mature student

John came for counselling for two years. He was 28 years old and was studying IT. Prior to coming to college he had been unemployed for a number of years. He was a hypochondriac, extremely anxious, and prone to extreme bouts of paranoia and persecution: if the IRA weren't out to get him, his lecturers were. He worked obsessively hard and veered between believing everyone in the class, including his lecturers, were stupid, to believing he couldn't cope, shouldn't have been taken on the course and should leave.

This pattern of behaviour lasted about a year, and it is fair to say that everyone found him a pain, including his counsellor. At first, the counsellor couldn't get a grip on John's world; there were many things he wouldn't talk about, especially regarding his family. He had great difficulty relating to others and he and his counsellor spent a lot of time looking at ways he could make friends, which meant looking at his effect on others and how critical and defensive he could be. Yet the more the counsellor saw him, the more she warmed to him: he was like a frightened deer and around every corner lurked a hidden danger. It took a year for John to trust the counsellor enough to tell her about his family situation, which was horrendous, and about being raped at school. From then on things moved with incredible speed. He left home, joined a sports club, learnt to play the guitar, fell obsessively in love with a girl who wasn't interested, recovered from that and passed his course with flying colours. He is now living with another girlfriend, unemployed and thinking of returning to college to do a Degree course. He will probably always be prone to bouts of extreme anxiety but he now has a greater understanding of his personality and therefore has more control over his over-whelming emotions.

Confidentiality

Counselling records often contain personal and sensitive information, which, if it found its way into the wrong hands, could be potentially damaging to the client. Counsellors have a responsibility under the Data Protection Act 1998 to ensure that client records are kept secure. Each counselling service will have its own policy and procedures for record-keeping and counsellors will need to make themselves familiar with these.

Sample policy

Record-keeping at a typical FE college

- Client notes are the property of the organisation; however, access is normally limited to the counselling team.
- Client personal details, such as name, age and address, are kept in a locked filing cabinet and are the only documents in the counselling office that contain personal details. Any letters, which are sent either to the client or to their GP, which contain personal details, will also be kept in this cabinet.
- Client counselling notes are kept in a separate locked filing cabinet and contain no personal detail. Students are advised that:
  - the counsellor keeps notes that are shredded when counselling ends;
  - they have a right to access these notes;

- the organisation has a confidentiality policy;
- they need to sign a working agreement to this effect.
- While most client notes are kept in paper form within a locked cabinet, letters to clients and their GPs may be kept on computer. Where any personal details are disclosed in a letter and kept on computer, the file is password protected.
- According to the BACP Information Sheet G1 (Bond and Jenkins, 2008, p6) there is no legal time limit for counsellors to keep notes so, in the absence of adequate storage space, we have decided that, in the interests of confidentiality, all notes should be shredded after a student has finished their counselling sessions. Records of their attendance will be kept for three years in a locked drawer in the counselling room.
- In the instance of a complaint being made against a counsellor or the organisation, the counsellor concerned will supply a report addressing the nature of the complaint. If the counsellor has left, then the Head of Student Services or another counsellor employed by the organisation will provide a report based on the available records.
- In the event that a counsellor becomes unwell and unable to continue work for a period of time, or in the event of death, the executor will take responsibility for the counsellor's client notes, i.e. destruction by shredding. They will also contact the counsellor's clients. The Head of Student Services will be the executor in this instance and will also take responsibility for any trainee or placement counsellor notes.

PROFESSIONAL QUALIFICATIONS FE COUNSELLORS NEED

Counsellors working in FE should have achieved a sufficient level of training and experience to be eligible for accreditation by BACP, COSCA, UKCP or the British Psychological Society (BPS).

They need to be experienced in working with both short-term and long-term clients and be able to demonstrate a real understanding of the issues that face many young people today. The AUCC *Recommended Framework of Good Practice for Counselling Services Working within FE and HE Institutions* (2004) further states:

> It is good practice for them to be registered or accredited and to have experience or training relevant to issues specific to the client population (e.g. psychology of learning, transitions, etc.).

RECENT CHALLENGES FOR COUNSELLING IN FE

Currently, there are grave budget constraints affecting many colleges; some posts have been frozen and some long-standing counsellors have been made redundant. In the last five years attitudes have changed dramatically towards support for students.

National statistics confirm that an increasing number of students experience mental health difficulties. In response to the government agenda to widen participation, it is crucial that we are able to provide effective support for students who have these complex needs. Healthy FE is a national initiative that will be Ofsted inspected; for more information, see **www.excellence gateway.org.uk.**

FE counsellors need to maintain very good contacts with outside agencies and need to be able to consult with or refer to, for instance, drug workers or eating disorder specialists. Often these agencies come in to colleges via the Enrichment programme or Connexions to talk generally to students. A number of our students come to college as part of a rehabilitation programme and may have their own key workers.

Sometimes, a successful outcome of counselling is that the student leaves and comes back the next year when their circumstances change or they move to another course. It is widely recognised that some students come to college specifically because they can get free professional counselling, often encouraged by medical or careers advisers.

Undoubtedly, students benefit most from one-to-one professional contact. Many of our students have no support from their family, and tutors are often too busy to give them the amount of time some of them need.

The question is sometimes raised by management of where counselling fits into the emerging agenda for FE and do counsellors still have a role to play? Ruth Caleb (2010) puts forward a strong argument in favour of in-house counselling provision:

> *In-house counselling services understand the institutional culture and are committed to its aims and objectives. It improves student experience of the institution and allows the institution to evidence accountability and duty of care to its community.*
>
> (Caleb, 2010, p15)

CHAPTER SUMMARY

This is perhaps the most turbulent time we have lived through in the history of counselling in FE colleges. Funding shortages and the recession mean that many services are facing cuts while demand for student counselling has never been higher. Increasing numbers of younger students, many with special needs, require ongoing support and counselling throughout their time at college. Many colleges have adopted a team approach consisting of the college nurse, the safeguarding officer, counsellors and mental health care workers. Emotional well-being is high on the management agenda and to ensure our students receive the support they need, counsellors should be familiar with local agencies, their waiting lists and referral procedures. Working with young students can be particularly challenging and counsellors hoping to work in FE colleges need to be robust and flexible, and able to respond to the roller-coaster world of this age group.

Our students can be totally defenceless, vulnerable, at the end of their tether, often with no meaningful support system. Sharing their path to a healthy recovery and, hopefully, academic success is what makes the job so rewarding. There are few other professions that enable one to get to know such a varied amount of people so intimately and, in my view, to have such a chance to have a real positive, long-lasting effect on someone's life.

SUGGESTED FURTHER READING

Association of University and College Counsellors (2004) *Recommended Framework of Good Practice for Counselling Services Working Within FE and HE Institutions.* Lutterworth: BACP.

Bell, E (1996) *Counselling in Further and Higher Education.* Buckingham: Open University Press.

Counselling in HE and FE from a psychodynamic perspective.

Jenkins, P and Bond, T (2009) *Confidentiality Guidelines on Reporting Child Abuse for College Counsellors and Psychotherapists in Further Education and Sixth Form Colleges.* BACP Information Sheet E6. Lutterworth: BACP.

Pattison, S and Harris, B (2007) *Research on Counselling Children and Young People.* BACP Information Sheet R5 (Updated 2009). Lutterworth: BACP.

ONLINE RESOURCES

www.papyrus.org.uk Papyrus – prevention of young suicide and the promotion of positive mental health and well-being.

www.rcpsych.ac.uk/publications Royal College of Psychiatrists 'Changing Minds' – mental health for ages 13–17.

www.studentdepression.org/ Students Against Depression – a website about depression by students for students.

CHAPTER 3

Counselling in Higher Education (HE)

Judy Moore and Ruth Roberts

CORE KNOWLEDGE

- The counsellor working in HE needs to be sensitive to the priorities of the institution as well as to the needs of individual clients.
- Many counselling services are still dominated by either psychodynamic or person-centred models of counselling, although cognitive behavioural therapy (CBT) is included by some services, reflecting the current national bias.
- Counselling services can be broadly separated into two models with subtly different purposes reflected by the nature of their work.
- In addition to what might be regarded as 'traditional' students who are school leavers studying full-time, there are also many non-traditional students who bring a wide range of presenting issues.
- A key issue that faces all university counselling services at this time is how to make best, and most appropriate, use of resources within the context of more refined provision elsewhere.

INTRODUCTION

The aim of this chapter is to introduce you to working as a counsellor or trainee counsellor in HE. This sector has undergone many changes in the last thirty years and the work of counsellors in HE has also changed and developed over that time, bringing new challenges and expectations. We begin by giving an overview of counselling in HE, followed by an outline of current trends and issues facing HE counselling services. We will illustrate some of these through examples of our work as counsellors at the University Counselling Service at the University of East Anglia (UEA). Although a number of university counselling services now include staff counselling as part of their provision, we have given more specific examples from student counselling as students form the largest client group and require more cross-service liaison. As 'signposting' – or directing the client to other support services within the university – is one of the key features of student counselling, we have given examples of this aspect of the HE counsellor's work throughout the chapter.

COUNSELLING IN HE

Counselling for students is now embedded in the vast majority of HE institutions as part of central student support services and an increasing number also now offer some counselling provision for staff. All HE counsellors will have undergone a professional training in counselling/ psychotherapy and will follow the ethical guidelines of their professional body. However, the counsellor working in HE needs to be sensitive to the priorities of the institution as well as to the needs of individual clients.

The institutional view of counselling in HE

- The counsellor is employed by the university or college in which she works and needs to work with clients in awareness of other parts of the institution, particularly those where the student is taught and other student services.
- Counselling is provided by the institution to enable students to complete their studies and to enhance their learning experience.
- The counselling service needs to reflect the values and priorities of the institution and to work in conformity with its practices and procedures.

For the counsellor who comes to the HE context from private practice or other organisational settings where the priority is simply the client, the institutional context can come as rather a shock. The counsellor in HE needs to be aware that she is working both in the interests of the client and for the benefit of the institution. Sometimes, this sense of dual responsibility can raise important questions for counselling practice and give rise to some of the main challenges for the HE counsellor. This is particularly so when financial pressure and self-funding mean that students are expecting more *of* their counsellor while the cash-strapped institution is expecting more *from* her.

The early years and development of counselling in HE

Counselling in HE has developed through many different strands over the past fifty years. Pressure for counselling for students grew from those originally working in student health who recognised in the 1950s and 1960s that there was a need for a broader, non-medical response to students' psychological and emotional concerns. Courses in guidance and counselling, based on the American HE model of provision, were run at the universities of Keele and Reading in the 1960s (Newsome et al., 1973); a full-time course in student counselling was launched at the University of Aston in 1971 and the first in-service training for student counsellors began at London University in 1972.

Bell (1996) identifies three main strands of influence on the development of counselling in HE.

1. Those who came from a background in psychoanalysis.
2. Those who came from a background in student health provision and lobbied for counselling for students.
3. Those who were influenced by the North American person-centred counselling model of Carl Rogers and the development of personal counselling in American universities.

Although HE counselling has now largely been removed from its early medical context, the legacy of those individuals who shaped the profession in its early days means that many counselling services are still dominated by either psychodynamic or person-centred models of counselling. This picture has shifted somewhat in recent years with the recommendation of CBT as the therapy of choice for mild to moderate depression and anxiety by the National Institute for Clinical Excellence (NICE) in 2004. Although the NICE findings have since been disputed (e.g. Elliot and Freire, 2008) and a broader range of talking therapies has been included in updated recommendations (NICE, 2009), many counselling services in HE have chosen to employ a CBT practitioner or practitioners.

In recent years there have been significant developments in terms of university welfare provision for students (e.g. Grant, 2009) and some of the work once undertaken by the counselling service in terms of study skills and general mental health advice, for example, is now dealt with by teams of specialists in other parts of student services. A key issue that faces all university counselling services at this time is how to make best, and most appropriate, use of resources within the context of more refined provision elsewhere.

SOME BASIC FACTS ABOUT COUNSELLING IN HE IN THE UK

Participation in HE

In 1997, the Report of the National Committee of Inquiry into Higher Education, colloquially known as the 'Dearing Report', recommended that the government prepare for an expansion of up to 45 per cent participation in HE by 18–30-year-olds by the year 2017 (National Committee of Inquiry into Higher Education, 1997). Twelve years on from that report, participation rates have increased to 30 per cent of all 18–30-year-olds – approximately 2.3 million students. In addition, in 2007–8, approximately 341,000 students from outside of the UK were studying in HE in the UK (**www.hesa.ac.uk**). The number of Higher Education Institutions (HEIs) in the UK is also increasing, with approximately 264 HEIs operating in the UK in 2005 (AUCC, 2007).

Types of counselling services in HE

Counselling provision in HE varies according to many factors, in particular, the size, function and financial situation of the institution. It is difficult to give a generic picture of the sector as services vary widely in terms of staffing levels, physical presence and the quantity and kind of interventions offered to clients. Counselling services can be broadly separated into two models, with subtly different purposes reflected by the nature of their work. These models can be seen in Table 3.1.

In reality, most services offer an amalgam of the two models represented in Table 3.1. However, the philosophical approach of a service in terms of the counselling modality or modalities offered is likely to influence the kind of provision offered.

Where staff counselling is included as part of the service's provision, its operation is generally supported by the university's Human Resources department.

REFLECTION POINT

The majority of counselling training courses focus on a single counselling modality and integrative approaches also often have specific models for working rather than offering a pluralistic toolbox of skills. Increasingly, however, counsellors in HE are required to adapt their work to the structures and demands of the institution – e.g. by offering time-limited therapy, one-off longer sessions, group sessions or preventative psycho-educational workshops as well as supervision for trainees.

Consider the nature of your own counselling training.

- Are you philosophically committed to a particular way of working?
- How might you need to adapt your practice for the HE environment?
- What kind of CPD training might you need to undertake?

Mission and purpose	Types of interventions offered	Location within the institution	Referral routes in and out
To enable students to be psychologically well enough to complete their studies	Time-limited; solution focused; goal oriented; CBT Focused group work; bibliotherapy; online and guided self-help Preventative initiatives – groups, workshops and psycho-education	As part of one-stop-shop student services May be physically located in the same building or discreetly elsewhere on campus	Tutors and advisers GPs Self Friends and family Referral onwards of clients with longer term, enduring emotional or mental health problems and particular learning needs
To enhance learning and personal development and to facilitate life experiences while at university	Time-sensitive; person-centred Open and closed therapeutic groups Couples counselling Preventative initiatives – groups, workshops and psycho-education	Autonomous service within broader context of student services. Usually located separately from other services	Self Friends and family GP Tutors and advisers Referral onwards of students with enduring serious mental illness and special learning needs

Table 3.1: Two models of counselling service.

ACTIVITY 3.1

Counselling service mission statements are often available to view on the internet. Look up two or three mission statements for different services. What clues do they give you to the nature of the counselling offered, the philosophical approach of the service and the relationship of the service to the institution as a whole?

The location of university counselling services

- In a *campus-style* university a stand-alone counselling service is likely to be located in separate premises. It will have its own reception and waiting area.
- In a *city-centre based* university the counselling service is likely to be found in one of the large admin or teaching buildings. Most counselling services have their own reception and waiting areas.
- A *one-stop shop* can be found either in a campus-style or city-centre based university. Here a central reception area serves many different areas within student services.
- *Staff counselling* might be provided within the counselling service building used by students, usually with staggered or protected time-slots so that staff and student clients wait in reception at different times. In a few instances staff counselling is provided in a separate building, generally within the Human Resources department.

REFLECTION POINT

Consider the implications for practice of the different physical environments in which counselling is undertaken.

- What are your thoughts about confidentiality when collecting a new client from a busy waiting room?

Although most counselling rooms are suitably appointed, counselling services are rarely located in purpose-designed buildings. As such, counselling rooms can vary from location to location. Sessional counsellors, who are often part-time, rarely have their own permanent office or personalised working space. Consider your own needs as a counsellor.

- Do you favour a particular furniture arrangement, e.g. sitting in the chair nearest the door?
- How might you adapt to working in a non-personalised space?

- Are you able to build time in your day to arrange the space to meet your needs and those of your clients?
- Do you need an extra chair for two-chair exercises or access to a desk for paper-based exercises?

SOME GENERAL FEATURES OF STUDENT COUNSELLING

Counselling for students at all HE institutions in the UK is free. The counselling service, together with all student services, is centrally funded. Counsellors are employed by the university and the counselling service is responsible to the university for the professionalism of its work. The counselling service is both a discrete service and part of a much broader team concerned with many aspects of student welfare. Cross-service usage within student services is common and most clients, particularly those who are living away from home for the first time in their first year, are likely also to be registered with the university medical services.

The likelihood is that at a university counselling service – whatever its context or set-up – you will be involved at some time in liaison with other professionals. University students are generally very open to this kind of contact between services and other individuals, such as the academic tutor, and this can come as a surprise to counsellors who are used to working independently or in other kinds of counselling agency.

COMMON PRESENTING PROBLEMS IN HE

Students encounter all sorts of problems while at university. These may be external issues affecting a person's ability to study or issues directly related to their academic experience. Respondents to the 2006–7 AUCC Annual Survey ranked 'Depression and Mood Changes', 'Anxiety', 'Relationship Issues' and 'Academic Concerns' as the four most common presenting issues.

Depression

Depression is the most common presenting issue for student counselling in the UK (AUCC Annual Survey, 2006–7). There are many reasons why depression is so prevalent in student life. The 'Students Against Depression' website (**www.studentdepression.org**) notes the following contributory factors.

- Rapidly increasing numbers of students attending university.
- Lack of control both in terms of students choosing university as a life path and the unstructured environment of university learning.

- A sense of inferiority and unfavourable comparison with others.
- Perfectionist or all-or-nothing thinking about attainment in HE.
- Lifestyle issues such as late nights, heavy drinking and poor eating that do little to support well-being and mood.
- Peer pressure and the need to establish new social networks.
- Chronic stress and life events.

Signposting issues

An understanding of the contextual issues affecting students is vital for working with presenting concerns such as depression. Many students, regardless of how long they have been at an institution, are often unaware of the range of services available to them. In addition to services on campus, clients can also be signposted to online resources such as 'Students Against Depression' (**www.studentdepression.org**) and other support groups or resources to help deal with their problems.

Anxiety

Many students experience anxiety at university, especially in relation to academic work (explored in more detail below). However, students also experience other types of anxiety which can be closely linked to the precipitating factors for depression noted above. Clients sometimes present with acute forms of anxiety such as panic attacks or other anxiety-based disorders such as Obsessive Compulsive Disorder or social anxiety.

Signposting issues

In such instances it might be useful to signpost the client to additional sources of help such as the GP or their academic adviser should special arrangements be required for exams or presentations.

Transition issues

The transition to university life can prove particularly stressful for some students, especially those arriving from a different culture. However, the experience of living away from home and forging new relationships can also be stressful for UK students. Equally, at the end of a student's university life, new anxieties might arise relating to moving on, entering the world of work and leaving behind the familiarity of formal education.

Signposting issues

It is useful for counsellors to have an understanding of transition issues and culture shock (for further information, see **www.ukcisa.org.uk**) and to know where students can find other appropriate help through signposting to the university careers service or the international students' officer.

Relationship issues

Over the last thirty years the student profile has changed significantly and UEA is no exception to this. In addition to 'traditional' students, who are school-leavers studying full-time, there are also many 'non-traditional' students who bring a wide range of presenting issues. Mature students might be struggling to balance their academic work with family responsibilities; many come to recognise the inadequacy of existing relationships as they forge a new identity through new interests and new friends.

Overseas students are adapting not only to a new course, but also to a new culture and often feel particularly isolated. They require particular sensitivity on the part of the counsellor who will need not only to be aware of nuances of language but also might need to ask the client to explain unfamiliar aspects of their culture.

Younger students may have difficulty forging new relationships or experience difficulties when sharing lodgings for the first time. Often, students experience significant relationships for the first time or leave behind important relationships at home. Issues around sexual identity and finding a partner are also frequent concerns.

ACTIVITY 3.2

Consider how you might work with the following clients and list any appropriate signposting issues and other sources of help to which you might refer the client.

a. Anne was a mature student completing her final year dissertation; she came to counselling because her marriage had broken down and she wanted to talk through her decision to leave the family home.
b. Pan was a Chinese student studying maths. Although he had passed all the necessary language proficiency tests before coming to UEA, he was finding it very hard to understand his lecturers and was falling behind with his work. Pan was very ashamed to seek help and had not told anyone he was struggling.
c. James was a second-year undergraduate who came to counselling after an acrimonious break-up with his girlfriend. James felt isolated and low as he and his girlfriend shared many mutual friends at university. He had failed to submit two assignments and wanted to 'get back on track' with university life.

COMMENT

We make the following suggestions for Activity 3.2:

a. Depending on Anne's circumstances, it might be appropriate to signpost her to RELATE for couple counselling. Occasionally, university counselling services also offer couple counselling where one partner is a registered student. If Anne's home life is affecting her ability to work, it would be appropriate to advise her to inform her personal tutor as soon as possible and to seek advice about her academic situation. Tutors may be willing to grant deadline extensions or postpone work until the stressful situation has improved. In the authors' experience, schools of study usually prefer students to act proactively to avert academic problems rather than have to mitigate failure after the fact.
b. Pan would be appropriately signposted to an International Students' Officer or Learning Enhancement Tutor for additional help with assignments and English proficiency. Again, this person would usually be advised to seek advice from his school of study regarding the late submission of assignments before the situation deteriorated further.
c. Depending on the severity of James' low mood, his counsellor might suggest that he also see his GP to discuss how he is feeling. The non-submission of work might further lower James' motivation and mood. Again, it would be appropriate to advise the client to speak to his personal tutor regarding the late submission of assignments and ways to remedy his academic situation.

Academic concerns

Students often present for counselling complaining of general work-related problems such as procrastination, work-related anxiety or a lack of motivation. In these instances, there may be several underlying issues contributing to a global problem. It is useful for counsellors to have an idea of the kinds of educational problems students might encounter so that they can be appropriately signposted for specific help when needed.

Signposting issues

Students presenting with procrastination or a lack of motivation may have poorly developed study skills and would benefit from referral to a study skills tutor. Many students do not have experience of the kind of selective and pragmatic reading required for HE assignments. They become intimidated and bogged down by long reading lists and lose belief in their ability to work at an appropriate level and pace for HE. In these instances, guidance on reading skills, planning and structuring assignments is useful and appropriate.

For other students, the concept of independent learning can be frightening and full of risk, especially when often the only feedback students receive is on substantive assignments that contribute to their final mark. New students are often unsure of the academic territory at university and are looking for hard-and-fast rules for working. Some present for counselling in high distress following their first experience of 'failure'. Counselling for these clients is often about understanding the meaning of failure, learning to trust themselves and accepting risk. The challenge for the counsellor in these instances is to stay with the anxiety and uncertainty of the client rather than to refer immediately to a study skills tutor or reference guide.

Academic members of staff are often the first to encounter a student's distress or anxiety and may recommend counselling as a way of managing problems. Alternatively, however, academic tutors may have no idea that a student on their course is struggling emotionally and/or academically. Often, a counsellor's only communication with academic staff is in the form of a memo or letter supporting a student's academic appeal or submission of mitigating circumstances.

Counsellors rarely communicate with academic staff unless there is a specific request from the client to do so. Occasionally, an academic department might request confirmation that a client has attended counselling as a condition of returning from intercalation or to repeat a year. Again, any contact of this kind has to be agreed with the client.

REFLECTION POINT

At certain times of the year, e.g. prior to the exam period or prior to the main submission date for dissertations and project work, counselling services experience increased demand for sessions. At these times, some students present for counselling when they are at the point of imminent failure. As noted above, clients often request a 'supporting memo' for the submission of mitigating circumstances to the board of examiners when appealing against an unfavourable academic decision or to request a deadline extension.

- How might you respond to a client's request for a supporting memo when the client had attended an initial assessment but then subsequently failed to attend their ongoing sessions?

RECENT CHALLENGES FOR COUNSELLING IN HE

Mental health and student well-being

In 2003, the Royal College of Psychiatrists' report *The Mental Health of Students in Higher Education* set out a series of recommendations for HEIs to manage the increasing numbers of students with emotional and mental health needs. These included, in brief, promoting and providing information about mental health to students; providing appropriate care through counselling services and developing networks with local health providers to ensure the smooth transition of care for those whose needs cannot be met by the institution.

Most HEIs have now appointed a 'Mental Health Coordinator' or 'Adviser' to develop this mental health agenda, to encourage good practice and increase awareness of mental health issues across the institution. The role of the mental health coordinator is also to develop links with local providers, including the Primary Care Trust, psychiatrists and the Community Mental Health Team (CMHT).

Some university counselling services have regarded the introduction of mental health advisers with suspicion, particularly because they take on an advisory role within the institution and liaison with medical professionals previously regarded as the domain of the counsellors. The reality is that, with sensitivity on both sides, the mental health adviser's specialist role frees counsellors to concentrate on those clients for whom therapeutic engagement is more possible.

Signposting issues

Counsellors need to have a good understanding of referral routes beyond their own service for clients whose needs are too complex or specific to be helped by the counselling service alone. Counsellors need to recognise and work within their own level of competence; not to do so risks reducing the student's chances of obtaining appropriate help and wastes valuable counselling resources.

Case study 3.1   John

John was a regular counselling client, returning to counselling one month after the summer vacation. At the first session John appeared very withdrawn and told his counsellor that he had stopped taking his anti-depressant medication. He had not engaged in any work since returning to university and reported that he did

---

not feel like 'going on any more'. It was also apparent to the counsellor that John was not attending to his personal hygiene and the client admitted that he was 'barely eating'. John said he did not want to die but could not see how to get better. John's counsellor thought he should see his GP as soon as possible. With the client's permission, the counsellor walked with him to the University Medical Service to make an appointment to see the duty doctor that day and also contacted the university mental health coordinator to discuss how John could be best supported in his residence and with his studies.

REFLECTION POINT

An important theme of this chapter is the appropriate use of limited counselling resources. Counsellors are increasingly required to consider which clients can be best served by counselling and who might be appropriately referred elsewhere for help. Counsellors need to make important ethical decisions about the nature of the counselling offered. Some of the key debates raised by HE counselling include the following.

- Is counselling in this context appropriate only for symptom relief and problem solving? Or is it also appropriate and possible to offer deep relational work leading to broader personal development?
- Alternatively, should HE counselling provide ongoing support for clients with mental health difficulties who do not meet the criteria for intervention by other services?

In terms of your counselling experience so far, and the theoretical model of your work, consider the following questions.

- Who, in your view, are the kinds of clients who can be best helped by counselling?
- What is the difference between counselling and crisis resolution?
- In what circumstances might you decide to take action regarding a client's mental health?

Learning disabilities

The last thirty years have seen a large expansion of the numbers of students entering into HE in the UK and during that time there has been much talk about 'Widening Participation and Access' to HE. The Higher Education Funding Council for England (HEFCE) defines the widening participation agenda as:

Ensuring equality of opportunity for disabled students, mature students, women and men, and all ethnic groups.

(www.hefce.ac.uk/widen/)

HEIs are charged with ensuring not only fair access to prospective students but also equitable treatment of students during the course of their studies. Following the implementation of the Special Educational Needs and Disability Act 2001, FE and HE institutions are required to make *reasonable adjustments* for students with a disability to ensure that they are able to participate in academic activities to the same level as their peers. The legislation also requires that, as far as possible, adjustments should be anticipatory rather than reactive and applicable to all aspects of HEI provision. It is therefore relevant to counselling as a part of student services. As part of their work in HEIs, counsellors need an awareness of equality issues in their work, especially with regard to learning disabilities and other 'unseen' disabilities such as dyslexia, Asperger's syndrome or ADHD.

Signposting issues

A basic understanding of the common indicators for dyslexia might prove invaluable for a client who presents with issues to do with organisation and time management. The underlying problem might not be apparent to the client who presents with a set of symptoms relating to their learning that are causing anxiety and distress. Counselling may enable a client to manage difficult emotions regarding learning but, where there is a specific learning difficulty, it is not likely to assist them in passing their course unless they are also offered practical, tailored help specific to their needs. A referral to a dyslexia tutor would be appropriate in this case.

Financial pressures

Apart from those from the wealthiest backgrounds, many students experience considerable financial pressure, often needing to engage in menial part-time paid work to supplement their income. (The recent case of 'Belle de Jour' also highlighted the fact that some students reportedly go to extreme lengths to support their studies.) In recent years it has also been recognised that students from non-traditional – which are often the poorest – backgrounds are the group that are in greatest danger of dropping out of their studies and require a particularly high level of support.

Most undergraduate students in the UK take out loans for both their tuition fees and for their living costs throughout the year. Some students from low-income families may qualify for a full maintenance grant, currently £2,906, but will need to supplement this by taking part-time paid work. Other students operate on a combination of student loan and parental contribution supplemented by part-time work. Postgraduate students may be funded by research councils and other charities, but many postgraduate students support themselves by taking out a Career Development Loan. At the end of their degree courses, therefore, most students end up considerably in debt. While signposting to Financial Advisers is part of the work of the student counsellor, financial pressure impacts more generally on students' well-being and often features as one of many concerns in counselling sessions. A recent AUCC article points out that *it is not uncommon for financial pressures to be a contributory factor in the emotional and academic decline of vulnerable students* (2007, p19).

Long-standing mental health issues and complex life circumstances add to financial pressures to make the experience of students from non-traditional backgrounds in HE particularly challenging. At the same time, the steady rise in tuition fees and the need for almost all students to take out some level of maintenance loan means that students increasingly regard themselves as consumers and have high expectations of the kind of service that they will receive.

ACTIVITY 3.3

- How might a client's financial situation impact the counselling process?
- What expectations do clients bring with them when they see themselves as university customers paying for their education?

GENERAL ISSUES FOR COUNSELLORS TO CONSIDER

Waiting times and counselling contracts

The demand for places can lead to pressure on services and inevitably a wait for clients for ongoing sessions; 63.5 per cent of respondents to the 2006–7 AUCC survey reported a 'significant waiting list' during the year.

For the year 2006–7, however, only 38.5 per cent of respondents reported that they imposed a limit on the number of sessions offered. This seems a relatively low figure given the reported pressure on sessions. The nature of counselling in HEIs would seem to preclude the need for long-term counselling contracts in the majority of cases. In 2003, the Royal College of Psychiatrists reported that the average number of sessions in HEIs was 4.5. There are many reasons for the brevity of this average contract, for example, the majority of students are only continuously present at their institution for short periods of time (between 8 and 12 weeks for most undergraduates). Also, student clients often experience relatively quick periods of change and progress with their issues. There are also many other factors as to why student clients are less likely to opt for longer term counselling. For example, students are often at university for relatively short periods of time with long breaks for vacations that can interrupt ongoing counselling relationships; client issues are often most pertinent at specific times during the year, e.g. during examination or transition periods and do not warrant longer term counselling; and termly timetable changes and extra-curricular commitments can also result in a temporary or permanent termination of sessions. The transitory nature of the student body also means that issues to do with relationships or interpersonal difficulties in shared accommodation can be resolved 'naturally' at the end of the year.

REFLECTION POINT

Consider your experience of counselling to date.

- Has the majority of your work been long or short term?
- What is your usual pace of working?
- Do you set goals and plan your work with the client or do you allow the client to set the pace and direction from session to session?
- What are the implications for practice when working with a limited contract of six or eight sessions as opposed to an open-ended ongoing contract?
- Given that HE counsellors often work to a limit of six or eight sessions, what issues might be discussed in supervision and case management regarding clients who require extended episodes of counselling?

Time boundaries

Many students at university find themselves in an unstructured environment where they have long gaps in their timetable for self-directed learning. On the other hand, some courses have very busy timetables which vary from week to week. Attending a weekly counselling session can therefore be a challenge to many students. Counsellors may find themselves having to renegotiate appointment times or agreeing to alterations in the frequency of meetings depending on the client's availability.

Where services operate a time-restricted counselling contract, the model used at most services is for a standard contract of six weekly sessions of 50 minutes duration, although research indicates that eight is the optimum number of sessions for short-term work (Cooper, 2008). Nevertheless, some flexibility is required for students who are on placements or for whom a tapered end to sessions will be most useful and for those who are particularly vulnerable or at risk, these boundaries have to be extended.

Counsellors also have to deal with the issue of non-attendance and frequent cancellations of sessions. Sometimes, this means ending a counselling contract with no satisfactory closure on the part of the counsellor. This can be an uncomfortable experience when the client was anxious or distressed but subsequently missed several sessions. Service policies will vary on this issue. Some services follow up a missed appointment by an email or telephone message and a provisional booking for the next one or two appointments. However, at peak times this might mean holding sessions that go unused when they could have been taken up by another client.

ACTIVITY 3.4

Write a list of the issues you might need to consider when terminating a counselling contract due to client non-attendance.

Personal boundaries

University counsellors sometimes have to negotiate interesting personal boundaries with clients. For example, counsellors may bump into clients on campus or when using university facilities such as the library, nursery or sports centre. Some counsellors have a blanket policy of never greeting a client unless first greeted by them. Others negotiate the issue of bumping into clients early on in their sessions or of necessity after a particularly awkward encounter.

Trainee counsellors who are also students at the institution where they are undertaking their placement might need to negotiate issues around partaking in campus social life – for example, being seen by clients in the union bar or attending the counselling service as clients themselves. Counsellors might themselves undertake study on part-time courses which clients might also choose to attend. Counsellors need to assess the appropriateness of participating in such activities, especially if the nature of the course necessitates self-disclosure or group work, while also balancing their own needs for CPD and self-development to gain or maintain accreditation.

Some clients develop strong feelings of dependence for their counsellor and experience loss and abandonment when sessions finish. Some may be very pleased to know that their counsellor is around on campus and may seek to prolong contact by inviting their counsellor to events such as art shows or drama productions long after counselling has finished.

Counselling in a small community

In 2007, the AUCC estimated that the ratio of counsellors to students in the UK was about 4650:1 (AUCC, 2007, as yet unpublished). The potential for overlapping relationships between clients and counsellors is, therefore, great. Counsellors might become aware that they are seeing clients who are housemates or course peers. Sometimes, clients are overt in wanting friends to see their counsellor and this may be discovered during the assessment session of the friend in question or mid-way through the counselling process.

Case study 3.2   Barbara and Jane

Barbara had seen Jane, a second-year student, for several sessions when the client announced 'Sally and I really think these sessions are helping. She tells me all about her sessions when she gets home but I don't really say much about mine. If I'm honest, I was a bit jealous when she started to see you too.' Until this point, the counsellor was not aware that the clients were flatmates as she saw them on different days and had never had occasion to use their contact details.

Confidentiality

All university counselling services abide by the ethical guidelines of a professional body such as the BACP. A copy of the *Ethical Framework for Counsellors* is generally visibly displayed and it is made clear that all counsellors subscribe to the principles of this Framework and that the service as a whole is run in keeping with its guidelines.

The counselling service in HE is a confidential service and clients can trust that no communication about them will ever be made without their explicit consent. In practice, this means that even if a parent or a member of academic staff rings the service to query whether or not a student is attending counselling, the receptionist would not give this information. Notes kept on individual clients are confidential to the service. Although communication with other parts of the university about individual clients is common, it is only done with the explicit consent of the client. The extremely rare exception to this is when a client is regarded as being an extreme risk to self or others and the counsellor might choose, having consulted with senior colleagues, to break confidentiality and inform the medical services or the student services department of their concerns.

Risk

The evaluation of risk is an important aspect of working with clients in HE and aids the counsellor to make decisions about onward referrals. Most counselling services have an agreed risk policy whereby the files of clients who report that they are 'at risk' are flagged in some way to aid awareness of reception and counselling staff. Each counselling service will have its own approach to risk and you will need to be aware of policies and procedures regarding dealing with suicidal or 'at risk' clients.

Signposting issues

The fact that a university counselling service generally exists as part of a broader network of support is particularly helpful when dealing with an at-risk or suicidal client. The client would normally be asked if they have discussed how they are feeling with their GP or one of the mental health advisers. If appropriate, the counsellor might then ask if the client would be willing for contact to be made with the GP so that the most appropriate form of support could be discussed. It is extremely important in all these cases that the client's permission is sought where possible, as this kind of liaison needs to operate within the strict bounds of confidentiality.

When working with an at-risk or suicidal client, it is also useful to ensure that the client has information about out-of-hours crisis services such as the Samaritans or the out-of-hours GP. Most counselling services have local resource lists or crisis cards detailing such information that can be given out to clients during sessions or made available to clients in waiting rooms and on the internet.

Research summary

Most counselling services engage in some kind of evaluation of their counselling practice and give clients questionnaires to fill out at the end of their counselling

---

process. Other counselling services engage in more systematic evaluation through computer-based systems such as CORE (Clinical Outcomes in Routine Evaluation). Qualitative data from questionnaires and quantitative data from outcome measures such as CORE can be included in the service's annual report to provide evidence of the usefulness and efficacy of the work of the counselling service to the broader institution.

REFLECTION POINT

- What experience do you have to date of using evaluative questionnaires with your clients?
- In terms of your own philosophical approach to counselling, what issues would you need to consider if required to routinely implement a measure such as CORE in your work?

PROFESSIONAL QUALIFICATIONS AND PERSONAL QUALITIES NEEDED IN A COUNSELLOR IN HE

Any counsellor wishing to work in HE will be expected have a degree plus a professional qualification in counselling, generally from a course accredited by BACP, UKCP, BABCP (the British Association for Behavioural and Cognitive Psychotherapies) or (in Scotland) COSCA. Other practitioners may be registered with the BPS (British Psychological Society) or BPC (the British Psychoanalytic Council). If they are not already accredited by their professional body they should be working towards accreditation and to have completed at least 450 counselling hours. They need to be experienced in short-term as well as longer-term work and be prepared to work within the constraints of a time-limited framework.

It is not necessary to have a degree in any specific subject, but it is very important within the HE framework that counsellors have good written and oral communication skills in order to communicate effectively with colleagues within the broader university community.

Counsellors in HE are often expected to engage in some kind of teaching or group work, whether it be running counselling groups, leading sessions on stress management or teaching mindfulness to students or staff. Sometimes, teaching will be done in liaison with colleagues from other departments, particularly other sectors of student services. It is therefore not unusual for 'teaching and/or training experience' to be listed as one of the 'desirable' qualities on the person specification for a new counsellor post.

Many counsellors in HE now hold a master's level qualification and an increasing number of counsellors are qualified to doctoral level. The most important thing, however, if you want to work in this particular kind of counselling environment, is to gain relevant experience, either through being on placement at a university or college counselling service or through seeking voluntary work in this area. It would be very unusual indeed to be employed as a counsellor in HE immediately after obtaining a basic professional qualification, even if that qualification were at level 7. Table 3.2 outlines essential and desirable qualities for counsellors in HE.

CHAPTER SUMMARY

Counselling in HE operates within a highly structured context and is, in most successful HE institutions, a recognised and valued part of university welfare

	Essential	**Desirable**
Education	A degree A Diploma in Counselling from a BACP (or equivalent) accredited course Individual accreditation by BACP (or other professional body) or working towards accreditation	A Master's degree
Experience and achievements	Experience of time-limited or time-sensitive work	Teaching and/or training experience
Skills and knowledge	Excellent written and oral communication skills	Specialist understanding of one or more counselling-related areas
Personal attributes	The ability to work collaboratively and cooperatively with a team The ability to work independently A willingness to work flexible hours when necessary	
Special circumstances		Experience of working in a HE or FE context

Table 3.2: Essential and desirable qualities for counsellors in HE.

provision for students and, in some institutions, staff. Counselling contributes to student retention and to the overall well-being of the university population. The counsellor working in this context needs to have understanding not only of the need for accountability but also of the broader structure in which counselling operates. In particular, the counsellor in HE needs to be aware of how and where to signpost students to other services when appropriate. As a counsellor in HE you are likely to find yourself negotiating a student's needs with colleagues in other student service departments or writing memos in their support to academic staff. Managing the boundaries of confidentiality within this context needs to be done with sensitivity and helping other colleagues within the university to better understand the role of the counsellor is an important aspect of the work of the service. You might find yourself participating in the service's evaluation and outcome procedures and perhaps writing a case study of your work for the annual report.

As universities nationwide face a funding crisis, counselling services are under great pressure: client numbers are increasing while resources remain either static or shrinking. Maintaining professional standards under this kind of pressure is an ongoing challenge for all counselling services in HE at this time. Students are themselves under financial pressure, amassing significant debt as they study, and the role of the counsellor in HE is increasingly one of enabling them to unpick the general sense of being overwhelmed with which they often present. The current challenge for the counsellor is to resist being overwhelmed herself: to understand when and how far counselling actually can help the student and when other resources – including those provided by the mental health adviser – are more appropriate. The counsellor in HE needs to work sensitively with the client and intelligently in terms of the client's context.

Students in HE, whatever their age, are in a state of rapid transition and their potential for growth and change is huge. Those who become clients of the counselling service are likely to benefit not simply in terms of improving their current situation but in developing insight, self-awareness and coping skills for the rest of their lives. For the counsellor, the challenges of working in the HE context are many, but the rewards, particularly in terms of the benefits to individual clients, are great.

SUGGESTED FURTHER READING

Association of University and College Counsellors (2007) Know the Territory – an overview of the UK higher education arena. *AUCC Journal,* March 2007: 13–20.

A concise overview of HE in the UK.

Bell, E (1996) *Counselling in Further and Higher Education.* Buckingham: Open University Press.

Counselling in HE from a Psychodynamic perspective.

Lago, C and Shipton, G (1994) *On Listening and Learning, Student Counselling in Further and Higher Education.* London: Central Book Publishing.

Counselling in HE from a humanistic/person-centred perspective.

Palmer, S and Puri, A (2006) *Coping With Stress at University: A survival guide.* London: Sage.

A useful book for students.

Peelo, MT (1994) *Helping Students With Study Problems.* Buckingham: The Society for Research into Higher Education and Open University Press.

Research into student needs in HE.

Raaheim, K, Wankowski, J and Radford, J (1991) *Helping Students to Learn: Teaching, counselling, research.* Milton Keynes: The Society for Research into Higher Education and Open University Press.

Rana, R (2000) *Counselling Students: A psychodynamic perspective.* Basingstoke: Macmillan.

Counselling in HE from a psychodynamic perspective.

ONLINE RESOURCES

For counsellors:

www.aucc.uk.com/ Association for University and College Counselling (AUCC).

For students:

www.student.counselling.co.uk/index.htm Student counselling in UK universities.

www.studentdepression.org/ Students Against Depression.

www.thestudentroom.co.uk Student discussion site.

For research postgraduates:

www.vitae.ac.uk/

For international students:

www.ukcisa.org.uk/

CHAPTER 4

Counselling in a voluntary agency

Cathy Austin and Kelvin Smith

CORE KNOWLEDGE

- Counsellors are expected to work to the same professional standards as the private and public sectors and to abide by the Ethical Framework of a professional body such as the BACP.
- Funding concerns are prevalent in the voluntary sector; these concerns can cause instability and threaten the work of agencies already operating within strict budgetary constraints.
- Counsellors seeking voluntary placements are usually required to demonstrate a commitment to undertake appropriate training, regular counselling hours, supervision and other duties before a placement will be offered.
- Counsellors may also need to agree to uphold the philosophical or religious views of the agency for which they work.
- Voluntary agencies work outside the normal multidisciplinary teams of the public sector. Counsellors need to be aware of referral routes and policies for dealing with clients at risk of their particular agency.

INTRODUCTION

This chapter will consider some factors relating to counselling in the voluntary sector through drawing on the history and management of one voluntary agency, The St Barnabas Counselling Centre in Norwich. The chapter will give an overview of how voluntary agencies have evolved over time and the kinds of challenges that face those who work in this sector. The ethos that permeates the voluntary sector is one of offering low-cost counselling to all regardless of race, creed or financial status.

Funding restraints are pervasive in the voluntary sector and many people – including both counsellors and admin staff – give their time voluntarily to bring counselling to the community. Whether paid or unpaid, counsellors, administrators, directors and volunteers in this sector maintain high professional standards to deliver the best service to clients. This chapter aims to demonstrate what you will experience if you join a voluntary agency either as a trainee or as an experienced counsellor. The chapter will consider what a voluntary agency can offer both counsellors and clients that cannot be found in the public or private sectors. Counsellors in the voluntary sector are unlikely to be well-paid and may not be paid at all, but working in a close-knit and supportive environment can bring significant rewards as well as significant challenges.

THE HISTORY OF COUNSELLING IN THE VOLUNTARY SECTOR

Voluntary sector counselling is undertaken by non-profit-making organisations. This sector is also called the third sector, the other two sectors being the public and the private.

The origins of the voluntary sector lie in the mid-nineteenth century when social reformers such as Lord Shaftesbury and Dr Barnardo founded organisations aimed to relieve poverty and provide education.

In 1948, the National Marriage Guidance Council was one of the first voluntary organisations to define counselling as its main activity. The Wolfenden Committee in 1978 identified several categories of voluntary organisations including:

- mutual aid organisations where everyone is unpaid, such as Alcoholics Anonymous;
- volunteer organisations which provide services with volunteer workers, such as the Samaritans;
- voluntary organisations which have paid and voluntary workers, such as Scope;
- private non-profit-making organisations which employ professional staff backed by voluntary helpers, such as Barnardo's.

Today, the voluntary sector contains many varied groups offering counselling to their clients. Tyndall (1993) writes:

The definition of poverty has been extended to include poverty of lifestyle and many counselling agencies have become charities on grounds that they relieve the stress and unhappiness associated with poverty of mind, body or soul.

(p3)

Voluntary counselling agencies offer personal counselling in an office, some visit clients' homes, some offer group support, telephone or email support or all of the above. Some employ full-time staff as counsellors, and some employ sessional counsellors. Many voluntary counselling agencies rely exclusively upon volunteer counsellors who undergo in-house selection, training and supervision with the agency.

ACTIVITY 4.1

Do some research into a voluntary agency in your local area.

- What is the mission of the organisation?
- What services do they offer?
- Do they employ any paid staff or rely entirely on volunteers?

Case study 4.1   The development of a voluntary counselling service

In the early 1970s a revival of the Christian Healing Ministry in Norfolk led to the founding of the St Barnabas Ecumenical Centre for Christian Counselling and Healing as a charitable trust in 1974. At the time, the Centre became increasingly popular with congregations often exceeding 100.

During the first 18 months of the Centre's existence over 130 people sought its help, having been referred by doctors, clergy, parish workers, the Citizens Advice Bureau, and on the personal recommendation of friends and clients. Over time the work developed steadily, with most people coming for help because of spiritual needs. The initial team consisted of 12 counsellors who undertook specific training and supervision in line with the Centre's philosophical and theoretical direction.

Since the 1970s, the Centre has evolved from a Christian-based healing centre to a fully professional and non-denominational counselling centre, having extended its remit to include more complex client work and employee counselling due to the increasing demands of society, demands that the public and private sectors are not able to meet.

FUNDING – AN ONGOING TASK

Finding the material resources to enable counselling provision in the voluntary sector has always posed a significant challenge. National Lottery Funding and private bequests have always played a significant part in this respect. In more recent years voluntary agencies have sought to supplement free or low-cost counselling by charging companies at commercial rates for counselling provision for their employees. Increasingly, agencies have also made use of counsellors-in-training or newly qualified counsellors who need to build up the 450 hours of supervised counselling practice required for accreditation. This arrangement is of mutual benefit to the agency and to the counsellors themselves.

Lottery funding

The National Lottery Charities Board is one of five bodies that distribute awards from the National Lottery's Good Causes Fund. From every £1 spent on the National Lottery, 28 pence is allocated equally between the five Good Causes identified by Parliament as Arts, Heritage, Charities, Millennium and Sport. See **www.lotterycentral.co.uk** for further information.

Counselling services in the voluntary sector may apply for funding from the Charities Board. These can be for substantial amounts, allowing agencies to develop and expand their activities in ways that could not be met through ordinary fund-raising. For example, grants can allow for improvement in physical infrastructure such as by making adaptations for disabled clients or generally improving the agency's premises to the advantage of clients and staff alike.

Grants can be made to fund various projects including training, development and recruitment, and are often tied to specific targets and service improvements. For example, in the case of St Barnabas prior to Lottery funding, the number of counsellors had hovered around 18 for some years. Lottery targets meant that expansion was required. At one point, the team briefly reached 28 counsellors but settled at around 24.

Lottery grants are often time limited and dependent on policy directives from government. In the case of St Barnabas, it was hoped that a further smaller grant from the Lottery Board would be a possibility at the end of the three-year grant period. However, by then, new funding distribution policies introduced by the National Lottery meant that this bid failed and the grant ended.

FINANCIAL CRISES

Voluntary sector funding became increasingly problematic in the early 2000s and some agencies reached a point of crisis, being unable to maintain running costs and salaries.

Voluntary agencies that are registered charities and possibly also companies limited by guarantee are regulated by the requirements of both the Charity Commissioners and Company Law. As company directors or trustees, individuals would face heavy penalties if they knowingly allowed 'trading' to continue past a point where existing creditors could no longer be paid. It is for this reason that directors and trustees exercise the kind of power over a voluntary counselling agency that a counselling service embedded in an educational or NHS establishment might experience from those who control the institutional budget.

DONATIONS AND BEQUESTS

Voluntary agencies often rely on the goodwill of individuals who are committed to the cause of the agency to provide donations or bequests. During a time of acute financial crisis, in the summer of 2002, a retired treasurer of the St Barnabas Centre died, and left a very generous legacy of £17,000 to the Centre that she had served so well and faithfully since its very early days. This legacy came at a time when the Centre was struggling to keep its head above water, and ensured the continuation of the Centre's work.

REFLECTION POINT

Many paid posts in the voluntary sector are based on temporary contracts due to being attached to particular sources of funding. Consider how this might colour your experience of working in this sector and how you might manage this aspect of such a role in your work with clients.

RESOURCING COUNSELLING IN THE VOLUNTARY SECTOR IN THE EARLY TWENTY-FIRST CENTURY

Throughout the UK in the early years of this century there has been a new focus on alternative ways of raising funds. The following are some of the means by which additional funding is sought.

- Clients are now encouraged to make a contribution towards their counselling, however small.
- Contracts for counselling with local firms are tendered for and corporate clients will be seen by experienced counsellors.
- Some counselling agencies supplement their income by running training courses, e.g. in counselling skills.
- Local appeals and fund-raising events are held and some agencies use a fund-raiser or have an in-house fund-raising team.
- Counselling rooms may be rented out to counsellors for use in their own private practice.
- Group rooms may be rented out evenings and weekends to other approved organisations.
- Increasing use is made of counsellors-in-training and newly qualified counsellors to supplement the work of the more experienced voluntary counsellors.

RUNNING A VOLUNTARY COUNSELLING CENTRE

There are many elements that need to operate efficiently and effectively to ensure a smooth running centre. All centres in the voluntary sector normally have some or all of the following:

- board of trustees;
- director of counselling;
- administration;
- reception staff;
- advisory Council;
- supervisors;
- a dedicated team of volunteer counsellors.

All of these need to work together in their different roles to deliver a professional service to clients. Reception and counselling staff may be either paid or voluntary, and usually there is a combination of both paid and voluntary staff. The trustees are responsible for providing business guidance and an organisation such as an Advisory Council is responsible for providing counselling and ethical advice. These roles may be combined in one board or committee to whom the Director will report.

Sometimes supervision is provided in-house and sometimes it is contracted out. It is usual for voluntary agencies to provide supervision (either individual or group) for its unpaid counsellors. Those counselling agencies which require their counsellors to be checked by the Criminal Records Bureau (CRB) normally pay for this to be done. Most voluntary agencies are organisational members of BACP and a few are accredited services. Most of the counsellors are likely to be accredited by BACP (or an equivalent professional body) or to be working towards accreditation. Some voluntary agencies offer additional training to their voluntary counsellors to help them fulfil the remit of the agency. For example, Cruse, a charity specialising in bereavement, offers a course in 'Awareness in Bereavement Care'. This course requires 60 hours of study and must be taken by all Cruse counsellors before they are allowed to work with bereaved clients.

THE COUNSELLORS

In recent years, more well-trained and well-qualified counsellors have been available to work in the voluntary sector and in most agencies a demanding counsellor selection process has been introduced. By 2000, counselling agencies in the voluntary sector had ceased to be a place where voluntary counsellors worked; rather, it had become a sector where professional counsellors gave their time on a voluntary basis.

Many counsellors work both in private practice as well as on a voluntary basis for an agency because they want to 'give something back' to society, but increasing numbers of counsellors are at the beginning of their careers, seeking to enhance their experience by taking unpaid work either during or shortly after the completion of their training. Consequently, there is a high turnover of counsellors in the voluntary sector as counsellors will usually find paid employment as a result of the experience they have gained.

With this high turnover of counsellors there is a need for careful induction procedures. The following list outlines the kind of procedure a new counsellor will need to undergo.

- Any volunteer counsellor will be asked to commit to a minimum of one year, during which time they will complete a six-month probationary period and agree to see at least three clients each week.
- The counsellor will have an induction with the centre administrator where processes covering client acquisition, room booking, supervision, admin, statistics, building safety and security are all discussed.
- The counsellor is allocated a room and a four-hour time slot of their preference. They can then select potential clients from the waiting list, obtain clearance for seeing these clients from their allocated supervisor and arrange to see their first clients.

REFLECTION POINT

Consider the points above.

- What are your thoughts about undertaking unpaid work and the time commitment usually required by agencies?
- What might be your motivation for undertaking a placement at a voluntary agency?
- Do you think that experience of a particular life event (e.g. bereavement) would make you a better counsellor for clients who are undergoing similar experience?

Most counselling services in the voluntary sector keep statistical records of service usage, which may be used for an annual report. At some agencies there is a requirement for all counsellors to submit a monthly statistic form; an example of a monthly statistic form can be seen in Table 4.1.

The returns can also be used to plot total sessions month by month and to compare these with previous years. It is also possible to factor in income and calculate average client contributions for sessions, which in turn are used as a comparison to monitor the annual budget targets. Summaries of

Client ID	Attended	Client cancel	Counsellor cancel	Did not attend	Planned break	
09/155	x					
09/168		x				
09/288				x		
10/123	x					
10/211					x	
Subtotal	2	1	0	1	1	5

Table 4.1: Monthly statistic form.

counselling sessions can be retrieved for counsellors who require proof of their completed sessions when statistical records are kept.

COUNSELLORS-IN-TRAINING

Some counsellors within the voluntary sector have many years of experience and hundreds of counselling hours, but voluntary agencies also provide placements for trainees, usually those who are in the last year of their degree or diploma. These serve a probationary period which involves additional monitoring and restrictions on the severity of client symptoms that they can tackle. Typical parameters for a trainee counsellor might involve being contracted to provide a minimum of three client sessions each week, a requirement to attend regular supervision group meetings, to have an external individual supervisor and to attend a review with the director or an experienced counsellor at the end of their first six months.

Case study 4.2   The selection of trainee counsellors

The director of St Barnabas writes of her experience in selecting trainee counsellors:
    'We only take trainees from accredited counselling courses and they have to be in their last year of training. When they come for an interview we look for passion, a sense of humour, an easy manner, confidence and knowledge of themselves and an ability to demonstrate an understanding of the lives of others. Our clients come with increasingly complex issues; our counsellors need to be

robust, able to enter the world of the often deeply distressed and isolated people who come to us for help. Strength of character and a warm and compassionate nature are more important than academic ability, but an understanding of the theoretical basis upon which they practise is crucial. We take counsellors from all different theoretical backgrounds and believe this creates a really rich environment to explore different ideas and philosophies. In addition, they are expected to attend our Community meeting once a month and any training or workshops we put on, on subjects requested by the counsellors. So it is quite a commitment for the trainee; they cannot just come and do their client hours and disappear.'

Case study 4.3   Supervision and review of work

The kind of review that a trainee might undergo after they have been with the counselling agency for a probationary period is described by the director of St Barnabas:

'After six months we have a review with the trainee and they are asked to make a tape recording of a session, transcribe ten minutes of it commenting on the case and the process and to write a short piece on how they feel they have settled into the Centre. The tape will be listened to by the counsellor's group supervisor and one of the other supervisors chosen by the counsellor. If the review throws up any difficulties or concerns, for example a tape which shows that practice is not satisfactory to either or both supervisors, or where feedback from the supervision group contains a number of concerns the following action takes place.

- The Director of Counselling is informed.
- The grounds for concern are given to the counsellor with copies sent to their individual supervisor.
- Another review will take place probably about three months later with the same two supervisors as before.
- If after the second presentation the supervisors do not feel confident in the counsellor's work, they will be asked to complete with their current clients and their contract with St Barnabas will be terminated.

This is a very rare outcome. The process is usually seen by the counsellor as supportive and educational. It gives them a chance to reflect on the quality and depth of their work and often to appreciate how far they have come in terms of confidence and ability.

After the six-month review the counsellor is able to choose their own clients and take on any out-of-hours or contract work and increase their case-load from a minimum of three clients. One of the joys of working with trainees is to watch them gain a real sense of themselves as a counsellor able to reach out and help another human being.'

REFLECTION POINT

If you are a counsellor-in-training, how might you view this additional scrutiny of your work?

VOLUNTEER COUNSELLING AGREEMENT

Most agencies will require volunteer counsellors, whether trainees or experienced counsellors, to sign an agreement such as the sample below.

Sample volunteer counselling agreement

The Centre offers counselling to adults, and counsellors have agreed to donate their time free of charge to enable the Centre to provide a high-quality counselling service within the local community.

1. The Centre
a) The Centre will provide counsellors with supervision and administrative support to enable them to respond to the needs of clients including:
   • personal accident and professional indemnity insurance cover;
   • accommodation which conforms to Health and Safety regulations and offers privacy and security;
   • written policies on issues concerning their activities within the Centre;
   • re-imbursement of authorised expenses necessarily incurred in the course of work undertaken for the Centre, supported by receipts where appropriate;
   • management or other staff on the premises at specified times;
   • a duty of care to the clients of a counsellor, should the counsellor cease acting as a volunteer for the Centre.
b) The Centre has clinical responsibility for the services delivered to its clients by its counsellors.

2. Counsellors
a) The Centre has the following expectations of its volunteer counsellors:
   • to be available to see three clients each week for sessions lasting between 50 and 60 minutes, for 42 weeks in a year;
   • to agree work with clients in advance with the director of counselling or supervisor. Clients will be allocated to counsellors at the sole discretion of the director of counselling;
   • to support the Centre for at least 12 months, but are free to withdraw their services at any time on giving as much notice as possible.

---

b) Counsellors will be required to adhere to the procedures and policies of the Centre, including those relating to the treatment of clients in the event of the counsellor deciding to withdraw their services. In this event clients will have the choice of continuing with them as an independent practitioner, or of opting to transfer to another counsellor at the Centre, in which case the Director of Counselling will make appropriate alternative arrangements.

c) Counsellors will be expected to observe the ethical practice of the Centre by:

- attending community meetings and group supervision other than in exceptional circumstances, in which case the Centre should be informed in advance;
- having individual supervision at least once a month with a supervisor chosen in accordance with the centre criteria for external supervisors;
- negotiating a confidentiality contract with the supervisor that takes account of the requirements of the Centre to maintain clinical responsibility for client work;
- taking part in counsellor training or community building days or part days as part of a wider commitment to continuing professional and personal development;
- complying with the Ethical Framework for Good Practice of the British Association for Counselling and Psychotherapy (as is required by the Centre's membership of that association), and in every respect acting so as to maintain the standards and reputation of the Centre;
- protecting the private and confidential nature of the work of the Centre;
- taking responsibility for appropriate action in the event that their personal resources may become depleted for emotional or other reasons, which may require them to cease to offer counselling for a period of time;
- submitting annually to the Director of Counselling a self-assessment document for both appraisal and audit purposes;
- working within the stated ethos of the Centre.

3. Administrative

- Counsellors will be expected to work within the times that management/reception are present, but may choose to work at other times provided that they have arranged joint cover with a colleague.
- Counsellors will be required to provide monthly statistics of work undertaken, and to carry out the requisite administrative and evaluation tasks at the beginning and end of each counselling contract.
- It will normally be the responsibility of receptionists to take client contributions before each session, but where this is not possible counsellors will be expected to collect them.
- Any matters of dispute with the Director of Counselling, Centre management, a supervisor or a colleague, which have not been resolved informally, should be raised promptly using the provisions of the Complaint procedure.

4. Relationship between the Centre and each counsellor

The obligations and duties of the Centre, and each counsellor respectively are assumed by the parties voluntarily and in good faith, and the full hope and expectation that the parties will at all times fully comply with them, with the joint aim that the Centre shall be able to carry out its work and deliver its service to clients in a competent and effective fashion.

The relationship of the parties is not intended to be, and shall not be taken to be, that of employer and employee, and this Volunteer agreement is not to be interpreted as a contract of employment.

I confirm that I have read this Volunteer Agreement.

Print name of counsellor .... Signature ....

ACTIVITY 4.2

If you are considering applying for a volunteer position, write down the reasons why you would like to work in this sector.

- Are you particularly motivated to work with a particular issue or group of clients?
- What personal qualities might you bring to the role?

THE CLIENT EXPERIENCE

First appointments are sometimes known as 'Intakes' or 'Exploratory sessions' and counselling agencies will usually have a team of experienced counsellors who undertake these sessions. The information obtained from the Intake session is intended to give a picture not just of client issues and background, but also of availability and counselling preferences, where the team is of mixed orientation.

This information is also used to provide a recommendation as to the level of counselling experience that the counsellor for each particular client needs to have. Once a client has attended their Intake session and has been accepted they are then presented to counsellors as prospective clients. In some agencies the clients will be allocated to specific counsellors by an experienced counsellor.

To maintain confidential records and to protect individuals, in most counselling services clients are identified only by an internally generated client ID and sometimes by their first name. Personal contact details are kept in a separate location and cross-referenced to their ID. The only point at which all this information comes together is on the client database which is essential for producing statistical data for the Service reports.

ACTIVITY 4.3

The following client profiles represent recent Intakes referred to the Centre.

- What considerations would have to be taken into account when allocating these clients?
- Would your training/life experiences enable you to feel confident working with these clients?

Sheila came because her daughter had died of a muscle-wasting disease six months ago. The enormity of it had just hit her. She was devastated.

Pam was frightened to go home as her son was violent and aggressive. It transpired that her husband had killed himself, another son had died of cystic fibrosis and another son had died aged three months.

Suzie suffers from depression and has been referred by her doctor. She was adopted when she was four years old and has always suffered from feelings of rejection.

Talia is an asylum seeker. She had belonged to a church in her country that was banned by the government. When she was 19 she was imprisoned, raped and tortured. Her brother was shot dead. Her asylum application has been turned down twice by the Home Office and she is on her final appeal. Her church is supporting her in this country.

COMMENT

The life experiences of some trainees often means that they feel comfortable working with clients who would normally be allocated to experienced counsellors.

In the above examples Shelia was allocated to a trainee counsellor who had been a nurse and who felt able to work alongside someone experiencing raw grief, which can be very challenging for any counsellor. Pam was allocated to an experienced counsellor as she had complicated grief issues coupled with the problems of dealing with a violent son and her profound feelings of guilt and hopelessness. Suzie was allocated to a counsellor who was experienced in working with attachment issues resulting from adoption and knew when and if to refer to a specialist adoption agency if that was deemed appropriate. Talia was allocated to a trainee counsellor who had considerable experience working with the Red Cross and had supported a number of women in similar circumstances, albeit in a different role.

LIAISON WITH OTHER AGENCIES

The voluntary counselling agency is part of the broader community. It does not have the direct referral routes or immediate network of support that is available, for example, in educational or NHS contexts. Knowing what other resources are available to clients in the locality is, however, an important factor in the work of a voluntary counselling agency. Sometimes the counsellor might be asked to write in a client's support or liaise with other agencies, as in case study 4.4.

Case study 4.4   Liaison with other agencies

Harry was referred to his local voluntary counselling centre by his GP because he was suffering from depression. He was 69 years old and had been divorced for some years and had little contact with his children. He felt isolated and lonely and was becoming increasingly paranoid about his neighbours who he felt were ganging up against him. His counsellor worked with him for nine months and in that time he became aware of how his rather defensive attitude to those around him increased his isolation and potentially evoked aggressive responses from his neighbours. He formed a good relationship with his counsellor and with the receptionists at the centre. His living conditions did not improve, however, and following discussions with Harry and his GP, his counsellor, in consultation with the Centre Director, wrote to the Local Housing Association to support his application to be considered for supported lodgings. He was accepted and moved in. His life was transformed as he became involved in a local art group and started helping out in a charity shop. He felt able to end his counselling as he began to make relationships in the community and contact with his children improved. It was important to him to know that he could return to counselling if he needed to.

EVALUATION OF THE CLIENT EXPERIENCE

Like other counselling services, those in the voluntary sector will seek to evaluate the client experience of counselling. Some use quantitative measures such as CORE or other outcome measures. Other services devise their own questionnaires and rating scales to evaluate different aspects of the client experience. Some of the following comments on the quality of their counselling were made by clients during a recent voluntary service evaluation exercise:

My hour session goes very quickly and I often have more to say. I often wish I could have either longer sessions or more than one session per week.

The sessions have set a structure for me to work to, which is helpful through the week.

**** has been a supportive, understanding and kind counsellor who is helping me come to terms with some complex and complicated issues. I do not feel that he or [name of service] could have done anything more as I have and continue to benefit greatly from my sessions.

OUT-OF-HOURS AND CORPORATE CLIENTS

The normal operating hours of most voluntary counselling agencies are from 9 a.m. to 5 p.m., but in order to accommodate clients who may be in full-time employment and cannot attend during the day, agencies may also operate an evening or early morning service. These clients are likely to be asked to make a contribution towards their counselling which may be a set fee or based on a sliding scale of their disposable income. Clients in full-time employment are usually in a position to pay more than the minimum and can therefore afford the higher charges for an evening appointment. Some agencies also have arrangements with companies and organisations that refer their employees for counselling. This additional revenue is used to subsidise clients that cannot afford the minimum payment.

REFLECTION POINT

How might you address the issue of fees with a client who, although working full-time, is seeking low-cost or free counselling?

LONGER-TERM CLIENTS

Many clients in the voluntary sector have multiple issues. For these and other people, the 'six-session' model of counselling may not be sufficient. Some voluntary agencies endeavour to offer long-term counselling to some clients, while recognising the impact this has on its financial resources, since it often happens that those most in need of counselling are often also on low incomes.

Case study 4.5   Katie

Katie was referred to the counselling centre by her GP – she was suffering from severe depression as her partner had recently committed suicide. At her Intake session she told the counsellor that she had been raped by three men two years ago and had been sexually abused by her father for most of her childhood. She was 24 years old and had never talked about any of this before although she had seen a counsellor when she was at school.

Katie was self-harming and had returned home to live with her mother who was being very supportive but was disabled and needed a certain amount of care herself. She could only afford the minimum contribution and the Intake counsellor felt that she would need long-term counselling.

REFLECTION POINT

What issues might you need to consider in supervision or case review when deciding to extend sessions beyond the usual contract?

MANAGING RISK

The risk that a depressed client may commit suicide is something that haunts many counsellors in the voluntary sector due to the chaotic nature of some clients' lives and the fact that counselling, unlike in other organisational settings, is not integrated into a network of support.

Almost all voluntary counselling organisations have an Intake system. Part of this process involves assessing what risk the client poses to themselves, others and to property. Most agencies have an agreed risk policy and the new counsellor needs to be aware of the policies and procedures in place.

Many counselling services ask for the client's permission to contact their GP if considered necessary. It is usual policy for the client's permission to be sought unless there are good reasons to break the bounds of confidentiality.

If a potential client presents with a very real risk of suicide, is dependent on drugs or alcohol or is taking very strong medication such that they are not able to engage in a counselling relationship, the voluntary agency is likely to discuss alternative forms of support available to them. The agency will also ensure that 'at risk' clients have access to out-of-hours support via their GP or mental health teams or have contact details for the Samaritans or other appropriate support groups.

Child protection issues need to be raised with the Social Services department or the police and/or the GP. The Director of the agency would normally deal with these concerns. Clients are made aware that if there are grounds for believing that they may cause serious harm to any other person or child the appropriate authorities will be informed. Ideally, the counsellor would inform the client that this action was to be taken.

Case study 4.6   The suicidal client

John was 24 years old and referred himself to the counselling centre for an Intake appointment. He had been to a number of other agencies, anxious to start counselling as soon as possible. He told the Intake counsellor that voices in his head were telling him to kill himself. He said that his GP had referred him to the psychiatric services but they would not be able to see him for some time and he was desperate. He was taking anti-psychotic medication and he told the counsellor that he was drinking heavily and his parents were pressurising him to move out. The counsellor felt very concerned about this young man and did not feel that the agency would be able to give him the kind of intensive support that she felt he needed at that time. The Director immediately contacted his GP (he had given his consent for the agency to contact his doctor) expressing concern about John and asking if he could be referred as an emergency to the mental health crisis team. The GP knew John well and agreed to do this. The Director then wrote to John explaining that she had contacted his GP as it was felt that he needed more immediate support than could be offered by the agency at that time.

This case highlights the need for counselling agencies to have good relationships with their local GP surgeries and a working knowledge of mental health care teams. It is also important that in situations like this clients feel their distress is taken seriously and that the door is always open to them to access counselling services in the future.

ACTIVITY 4.4

Voluntary agencies often work in isolation in comparison with the multidisciplinary working found in other sectors. Considering this factor, make a list of the information you might need to know about your client to ensure that you are able to work safely and most effectively.

THE ROLE OF DIRECTOR IN A VOLUNTARY COUNSELLING CENTRE

The role of the Director is primarily to ensure that the counsellors are well supported. The Director needs to have not only a wide experience of counselling but a good knowledge of training courses from which trainees might be drawn and training possibilities for their own counsellors. They need to get to know each counsellor, their strengths and weaknesses, their preferred areas of working and their special interests. Stressed counsellors are not a great deal of help to anybody, so the Director needs to ensure as far as possible that counsellors are looking after themselves.

The Director aims to create an environment that enables a counsellor to have a sense of belonging. The Director needs to model good support and be open-minded, non-judgemental and compassionate, while maintaining the highest possible professional standards. Other duties often include doing Intake interviews and ensuring that new clients are seen as soon as possible after their initial enquiry. Allocating clients to counsellors involves knowing the counsellors' strengths and weaknesses and requires a certain level of experience. This ensures that both client and counsellor are as well matched as possible. Recruiting and interviewing counsellors is a time-consuming but obviously important part of the job.

The Director needs to ensure that the counsellors are safe and not alone in the building and have had an induction with the Administrator. He or she is expected to attend trustee meetings and produce a report, to meet with the supervisors and, if there is one, the Advisory Council on a regular basis. The Director is also expected to handle any complaints against the counselling centre and the counsellors, and review and up-date centre procedures and practices.

It is also vital that the Director is aware of local networks and be in touch with other counsellors and counselling agencies in the locality.

Support at a local level

In May 1999, the Director of St Barnabas met with the counselling co-ordinator of Off the Record, another voluntary counselling agency in Norwich. This marked the beginning of efforts to bring together counselling organisations in the city to speak jointly on behalf of their clients and counselling generally. By 2004, an organisation called ANCA (Association of Norwich Counselling Agencies) came into being as a result of this small beginning.

CHALLENGES FOR THE FUTURE

Even if a voluntary counselling agency has charitable status, it is never-theless entirely responsible for its own funding. GPs are now generally unable to offer counselling, other than through IAPT (see Chapter 8 for more detail) and this has increased the numbers referred to the voluntary sector. The severity and diversity of problems for which people are seeking help demands ever more resources from the counsellors and supervisors who work at the centre.

Although the voluntary sector has had to meet a number of challenges in the last few years, a lot of positive energy has emerged. Voluntary agencies have provided a professional counselling service to an increased number of clients.

Without dedicated staff, volunteers, trustees, friends and supporters, however, counselling in the voluntary sector could simply not exist, let alone flourish as it is doing in many areas. The voluntary sector remains one of the most rewarding places for a counsellor to find employment, whether it be at the beginning or the end of their career.

CHAPTER SUMMARY

The voluntary sector offers many important opportunities to increase the uptake of counselling in the community for a client group whose needs may not be met by the public or private sectors. These needs are increasingly prevalent with increased demand placed on public services and the reduced ability of many people to pay for services such as counselling.

Many counsellors take up unpaid employment with voluntary agencies either out of altruistic intentions to 'give something back' or to gain important experience at the beginning of their careers. Paid employment in this sector is often temporary and there is competition even for unpaid counselling positions. Counsellors may need to work beyond the confines of their counselling rooms, getting involved in the day-to-day running of centres, fund-raising or the promotion of their work in the community. Agencies sometimes specialise in working with particular groups of people. Increasingly, however, agencies are required to increase their remit and take on more lucrative work to support their charitable aims. Counsellors in this environment may encounter clients from very different walks of life. Despite funding difficulties, uncertainties about the future and often a quick turnover of voluntary staff, agencies have successfully developed procedures and standards to ensure the professionalism of their counsellors and the quality of the service offered to clients.

SUGGESTED FURTHER READING

Tyndall, N (1993) *Counselling in the Voluntary Sector.* Buckingham: Open University Press.

This is a useful introduction to the voluntary counselling sector in the early 1990s and explains the history of this work.

ONLINE RESOURCES

www.acevo.org.uk The Association of Chief Executives of Voluntary Organisations – represents the third sector at government level and offers support to individual agencies.

www.voluntarynorfolk.org.uk This local organisation gives a list of voluntary agencies in the area and job possibilities and opportunities. All areas nationally will have similar websites.

www.voluntaryworker.co.uk This is a national website with articles and details on how to find and participate in voluntary work.

CHAPTER 5

Addictions counselling in a residential treatment centre

Steve Roberts

CORE KNOWLEDGE

- 'Addictions counselling' is a unique form of counselling treatment which can be practised by counsellors from many different orientations where they possess a willingness to learn a new specialism.
- Self-care is of utmost importance to counsellors working in this field.
- Addictions counsellors need to work as part of a multidisciplinary team and be prepared to liaise with the different agencies involved in a person's care.
- Confidentiality is not usually held between the patient and their counsellor. In a residential setting, confidentiality is maintained between the patient and the multidisciplinary team.
- Addictions counsellors need to adjust their work to fit with the tasks of residential addictions therapy, which often necessitate directive ways of working and the use of a care plan approach.
- Counsellors may find themselves challenged to deliver and facilitate new methods of working, such as in groups, lectures and creative activities.
- The twelve-step approach is often the underpinning methodology in many treatment centres.

INTRODUCTION

The aim of this chapter is to prepare you to take up a placement or employment in the field of residential drug and alcohol treatment. After reading this chapter you should have an appreciation of what counselling in this field consists of, the practical experience recommended and the qualification routes laid out by the Federation of Drug and Alcohol Professionals. Most importantly, this chapter provides an overview of residential addiction treatment and highlights the day-to-day challenges of working in a treatment centre.

Like many applications of counselling, addictions therapy is a specific and discrete specialism. No generic qualification in counselling can possibly provide a thorough grounding in every specialism, and this chapter should help you to reflect on your current practice in the light of what is required in the drug and alcohol field. It will allow you to identify training shortfalls and signpost you towards further training opportunities.

Addictions counselling is not restricted to residential treatment. Government strategy aims for the de-escalation of problematic drug use at the earliest opportunity, beginning with education, progressing through youth work, community awareness projects, and local alcohol and drug services (often third sector providers or charities). Typical counselling-related interventions offered in this arena are controlled drinking advice and harm minimisation, as well as supportive and motivational counselling.

The difference between these services and 'formal treatment' is generally the requirement for complete abstinence from the problematic substance due to the harm being caused to the user and to people around them. 'Formal treatment' is usually accessed through NHS Trust alcohol and drug services and involves community detoxification and formal day pro-grammes. For those who are not able to manage their sobriety in the community (even with the help of family and professionals) the remaining option is residential treatment.

Addictions counselling is a highly rewarding endeavour. Clients may arrive in treatment looking as though they have stepped out of a war-zone. Witnessing a person rebuild themselves physically, emotionally, mentally and perhaps even spiritually, is a humbling experience. However, the success rate across the field remains poor overall and, for every success story, there are greater numbers of near misses, outright failures and, even, tragedies. A retrospective study of over 26,000 anonymous drug users in a variety of treatment settings in the north-west region of the UK reported a 'discharged drug free' rate of just 3.5 per cent and a re-presentation to treatment rate the following year of 44.5 per cent for those who were discharged drug free (Beynon, 2006, p1).

Worryingly, the same can also be said for some addictions therapists. Many have trodden a well-worn, if heroic, path of attempting to help others, only to fall by the wayside through unrealistic expectations, poor self-care and emotional burnout.

Clients in residential treatment (like those suffering with addiction generally) are notoriously difficult to treat. Residential treatment can amount to little more than survival for the client and a preparation for a return to their challenging world. This is in contrast to counselling training that focuses on the development of the person from illness to health, or from emotional or mental stuckness to emotional and mental freedom (depending on your training orientation). It cannot be overestimated how radically different counselling for these clients is from conventional therapy. For the newcomer to this field, the difference is immediately felt both in terms of the extreme (and often distressing) condition of patients and the intensity of the treatment community itself.

In the short term, patients' objectives are specifically related to immediate improvement in their personal circumstances. One study into the reasons why patients seek residential treatment showed that improving self-understanding, improving mood or increasing personal effectiveness were not among respondents' primary goals (see research summary below). However, this is not to say that service users do not seek such goals in the long term or once their treatment has started.

Research summary

Why do individuals request residential treatment?

- Stop taking all drugs – 72 per cent
- Stop taking specific drugs – 12 per cent
- Reduce the level of overall drug use – 5 per cent
- Improve health – 21 per cent
- Improve employment chances – 19 per cent
- Improve relationships – 17 per cent
- Improve finances – 11 per cent
- Improve accommodation, access to their children or to benefit a family member – 10 per cent

(Jones et al., 2007, p11)

PURPOSE AND AIMS OF COUNSELLING IN A TREATMENT CENTRE

'Addictions counselling' as a unique form of counselling in its own right came into being in the 1970s (Powell and Brodsky, 2004). Therapists in this field are generally known as Addictions Counsellors, though the same practitioner may work in other fields concurrently under a different title. Some therapists provide a specific service in a residential setting, e.g. Cognitive Behavioural Therapy or Family Therapy. Other therapists might consider themselves to be Person-Centred or Integrative but the work they undertake in this setting might not be easily recognised as such by other practitioners from their orientation.

Residential treatment is, for the majority, a final attempt to get clean after a series of unsuccessful attempts 'in the community'. This is primarily due to the fact that residential treatment is very expensive (NTA, 2003). Other than highly exclusive treatment centres, the cost of rehabilitation typically varies from £500 per week at the lower end to £4,000 (at the higher end) with detoxification prices starting at £1,000 per week.

Residential treatment allows the patient to stop using their substance of choice in an environment where they can rely heavily on others for support and which is, by and large, free from illicit substances. Few patients find treatment an enjoyable experience. It is, after all, inherently stressful to experience thoughts, emotions, sensations and memories without the 'buffer to reality' that is the patient's substance of choice. Surprisingly, however, few apparently find it difficult to abstain while in treatment, a fact that highlights the importance of social and environmental factors in addiction. Crucially, residential treatment also gives patients a window of opportunity in which to prepare themselves for continued abstinence and recovery after their discharge.

Treatment usually follows a reasonably predictable formula of applying well-used interventions to help the individual achieve their goals. The interventions applied, together with patients' goals, can best be described as the tasks of treatment.

The tasks of treatment usually include most of the following:

- detoxification and support during withdrawals;
- healing and recovery from associated physical health complications;
- reflection on personal addictive processes and the effect they have had on their lives and the people in them (coming out of denial);
- coming to terms with the past and present, and leaving behind shame;
- learning to take responsibility for past, present and future actions;
- making important life decisions – especially the one to remain abstinent from their substance of choice;
- learning more about the causal and perpetuating factors of addiction and the pitfalls of early recovery;
- identifying and addressing underlying psychological factors that underpin the addictive process;
- regaining self-respect and confidence;
- addressing specific and/or general fears associated with 'normal' living, e.g. finding employment, managing relationships;
- addressing non-using but related behaviours, e.g. offending behaviour, co-dependency, workaholism, etc.;
- learning how to undertake tasks associated with everyday living without the need for substances (commonly known as 'rehabilitation').

In addition, residential treatment centres are required to provide education on harm minimisation and facilitate continuity of care by following through discharge plans.

TREATING ADDICTION

As noted above, treatment usually consists of applying various pre-chosen interventions. The World Health Organization's International Classification of Diseases version 10 Classification of Mental and Behavioural Disorders (ICD 10) diagnosis of substance misuse is far from straightforward, including separate diagnostic criteria for alcohol, all the main drug types and multiple drug use. Within each, there are separate diagnoses for acute intoxication, harmful use, dependence, withdrawals (with or without delirium) and associated amnesic or psychotic symptoms (ICD 10 2007 v Mental and behavioural disorders due to psychoactive substance use (F10-F19)) (WHO, 2007).

A consultation with a psychiatrist to establish the presence or otherwise of a secondary psychiatric condition (dual-diagnosis) is common in residential treatment. However, even single diagnosis substance misuse is frequently more obvious to the observer or family member than to the sufferer themselves.

Most people accepting treatment for substance misuse do so because they are no longer able to manage their lives and because they are causing themselves considerable physical harm. Additionally, their substance misuse may be having harmful social effects, e.g. on their family. Patients may choose treatment themselves, be coerced or persuaded by family members or even be legally obliged by the hand of the law (in the case of those referred for treatment through the criminal justice system).

PATIENT PROFILES AND REFERRAL ROUTES

Patients are referred to residential treatment through a variety of routes. Some may have a concerned family member who has arranged treatment and funding independently. Others may have sought funding from their local Drug and Alcohol Action Team (DAAT). These patients will usually have tried other interventions unsuccessfully before public money is spent on expensive residential treatment. Others may have had their treatment funded and organised by the probation service.

Where substance misuse is linked to criminal activity (often referred to as offending behaviour), patients may find themselves hurried into treatment for the good of the local community. Many such patients are subject to a Drug Rehabilitation Requirement (DRR), which has replaced the old Drug Testing and Treatment Order (DTTO). Up to 39 per cent of service users admitted to acquisitive crime in the four weeks prior to commencing treatment. Others, who are regarded as less of a 'threat to society', may have waited much longer for the opportunity of residential treatment (Jones et al., 2007).

Some patients will see treatment as a long-awaited opportunity to come off substances in a supportive environment while others may see treatment merely as a punishment or an extension of their prison sentence. It is fair to point out that while most patients do wish to stop misusing substances at some level, some have little or no intention of doing so and may even attempt to bring substances into treatment. Additionally, patients will have vastly differing objectives for treatment. Some will intend long-lasting, complete abstinence while others, for example, will only intend to stop using drugs and continue using alcohol.

THE ADDICTIONS THERAPIST IN A MULTIDISCIPLINARY TEAM

A counsellor who is new to addictions counselling will immediately notice two major differences from 'conventional' counselling.

First, the addictions counsellor does not work alone. In the vast majority of institutions, the addictions counsellor is part of a multidisciplinary team. Typically, the team will include a psychiatrist, GP, mental health nurse, general nurse, counsellor and support worker. All have a vital role within the team. It comes as a surprise to some that confidentiality is not held between the patient and counsellor. In a residential setting, confidentiality is maintained between the patient and the multidisciplinary team. As a focal point for the patient, it is essential that you, as therapist, communicate this to your patient as early as possible. Patient disclosures may have to be discussed in staff handover meetings as well as in case management meetings. It is usually possible to share critical information without causing undue embarrassment to your patient. For example, it is usually sufficient to explain to colleagues that they have disclosed significant childhood sexual abuse but not share specific details.

Second, the patient's treatment is carefully delivered according to their care plan following an in-depth assessment. Patients entering treatment normally have a complex array of physical, mental and emotional problems. Some are generic – for example, the need to develop relapse prevention strategies. Others are specific to each patient – for example, the need to monitor and treat deep vein thromboses caused by needle use or to address issues of abuse or relationship problems.

The requirements for residential treatment are clearly laid out by the National Treatment Agency (NTA, 2003), including developing, managing and reviewing written care plans, which (among other factors):

- set the goals of treatment and milestones to be achieved;
- indicate the interventions planned and highlight the professionals responsible for carrying them out;
- make explicit reference to risk management and identify the risk management plan and contingency plans;
- reflect the culture and ethnic background of substance misusers as well as their gender and sexuality.

Care plans vary in complexity but, at their most basic, include the fundamentals shown in Table 5.1.

Identified problem	Treatment goal	Intervention planned	Professional responsible	Review
Infected ulcers on left leg	Heal ulcers	Clean, dress and monitor infected ulcers	General nurse	Ulcers successfully healed (date)
Persistent relapse on return to community	Patient to understand personal relapse triggers and develop personal relapse prevention plan with counsellor	Relapse Prevention Group produce Personal Relapse Prevention Plan with support of counsellor	Counsellor	Personal Relapse Prevention Plan written (date)

Table 5.1: Sample care plan.

Working in a multidisciplinary team

- Patients should be made aware that confidentiality is shared within the multidisciplinary team from the outset.

- The therapist must remain respectful of their patients' dignity when sharing clinically significant information and should only discuss relevant details for the specific purpose of identifying care plan changes or vital exchange of information.
- Staff handover meetings are designed to benefit patients. Therapists should process their difficulties or frustrations within the context of supervision.
- Every member of the multidisciplinary team has a vital role to play – nobody has sole responsibility for the patient.

REFLECTION POINT

- How would you feel about confidentiality being held within a whole team of people rather than simply between you and your client?
- If you have trained in non-directive therapy, how would you feel about bringing an agenda to the counselling interaction as part of the patient's treatment plan?

TYPICAL INTERVENTIONS IN A RESIDENTIAL SETTING

Some treatment centres operate a purely twelve-step, abstinence-based programme while others favour cognitive or other methodologies. However, many offer an eclectic approach with the twelve-step methodology providing the core of the programme with specific interventions available according to individual needs. Most centres operate a core timetable of groups and lectures with free time that may be used for one-to-one interventions. A typical programme will include the following.

Assignment work

Most centres set their patients assignments which are designed to help facilitate self-reflection and understanding of their condition. A common first assignment is the 'Life Story' or 'Time Line' which tracks the development of addiction. Further assignments commonly follow the format of the twelve-step programme of Alcoholics Anonymous or use the CBT model to encourage understanding of addictive processes and the alternative thinking and behaviours that are identified for clean or sober living.

Group therapy

Groups usually last an hour at a time. Group time frequently follows a formula such as a brief reading (reminding individuals of the nature and purpose of the group), a feelings check, and time to process emotions and thoughts in the group setting. This time may also be used for reading assignment work to peers and receiving feedback.

Case study 5.1 Sarah

Sarah reads her first assignment to the group. Having written it without assistance, this is the first time she has publicly disclosed her feelings and actions and she feels overwhelmed by her emotions. The other group members' initial reaction of discomfort gives way to compassion and then admiration. Sarah insists on completing her task despite her distress and she gains strength from the encouragement of her group. Some feel the need to identify with Sarah and share their stories too. By the end, all of the group feel drained but inspired.

Community groups

The community group is a space in which issues affecting the whole community may be aired and collective decisions made. Commonly, community meetings are held at the beginning and end of the day with time for individuals (including staff) to state their goal for the day and, later on, reflect on their progress. As in any home, disagreements are common and need to be aired.

Case study 5.2 Claire and David

During the evening a small change bag containing a patient's weekly allowance (£10) has gone missing. Claire, who has lost the money, blames David with whom she has already had disagreements. Accusations and insults are traded as other members of the community join in and the meeting erupts into shouting and arguments. David gets out of his seat and refuses to sit back down as he verbally confronts Stuart who has accused him of preying on vulnerable women. Helen, a middle-aged woman who arrived in treatment only yesterday, becomes tearful and distressed while David has to be restrained by other male patients. Eventually, David leaves the community room and the sound of breaking windows can be heard from the adjacent corridor.

Art/music/creative therapy

Creative therapies have long been established in addiction treatment as a means of expressing deeply hidden and painful emotions. They also provide the opportunity to engage with a positive activity or to have some light relief from endless talking and encounter. Some centres have published drawings, paintings, poetry and songs created by their clients: for example, a selection of mixed media art can be viewed on the Castle Craig Hospital website (the URL can be found in the online resources section at the end of the chapter). Where musical instruments are provided, bands may spring up or patients may learn an instrument and, in doing so, discover new ways to express themselves or to manage their mood. Some creative expression using musical instruments (for example, drums) has been reported to assist in inducing relaxation, a sense of connectedness with self and others, and alleviation from isolation (Winkelman, 2003).

Individual therapy

Individual therapy may seem, on the face of it, to be the one part of treatment for which a newly qualified counsellor is thoroughly prepared. However, therapy in a treatment centre varies considerably from 'conventional' counselling. In this setting, therapy takes place within the patients' own (temporary) home. As the therapist, you work with the patient in their home (albeit in a specific counselling room) rather than the patient coming to you. Furthermore, individual therapy is just one part of the treatment experience and the patient may not particularly want or value it. In an effective establishment, which wholly embraces the care plan approach, the content and purpose of individual therapy is likely to have been identified at the outset. For example, it may be to help the client learn mechanisms for impulse control, anger management, to process trauma or learn new skills to manage anxiety or depression.

It is rare for individual therapy to be wholly unstructured and to follow classical person-centred principles. The scope of this chapter does not allow for an in-depth examination of therapeutic modalities in respect of addictions. However, it is worth pointing out that most sufferers of addiction have become wholly unused to taking personal responsibility and, as such, expecting patients to play an active role in their therapy without intervention and guidance from the therapist is generally unrealistic. This being said, while the form of individual therapy may differ, the underpinning factors of Rogers' Core Conditions of unconditional positive regard, empathy and congruence remain absolutely vital during individual therapy whatever form it takes (NTA, 2006).

Even in the absence of specific goals for one-to-one therapy, the patient will usually have assignment work to do, and will seek advice and assistance for it with their counsellor. Commonly, patients will be assigned a therapist who will be their 'key worker' throughout treatment. Where good rapport is established, collaboration generally emerges, with individual therapy used by patients to continuously plan and review their treatment experience as well as to meet specific care plan objectives. In contrast to 'conventional' counselling, if rapport is *not* established, the patient is not usually able to change to another therapist and is therefore 'stuck with you'. In these cases, patients may simply fail to show up for therapy while others may confront you plainly and bluntly with their dissatisfaction!

ACTIVITY 5.2

Jade comes to see one of the therapists in the general office and complains that her counsellor is 'textbook' and doesn't understand what it is like to be addicted. She says her counsellor just wants her to write assignments and won't do anything else to help her. She asks if you will be her therapist as you understand her better and know when to stop pushing with assignments!

- How would you respond to Jade?
- What might you say to her counsellor?

COMMENT

In situations such as Jade's, it is useful to ask patients to describe what they wanted to say to their therapist that they felt was not being understood and then to encourage them to repeat it to their own counsellor. The outcome was motivating for the patient as they used their own resources to solve their problem without undermining their therapist in any way.

Lecture programme

This will include vital knowledge on recovery from substance misuse, including physical health information and advice. Health information may include harm minimisation, hepatitis and other blood-born viruses and sexual health. Subjects on recovery-related matters may include: managing relationships and avoiding co-dependency; maintaining personal boundaries; identifying triggers; handling cravings; building support networks and setting goals for the future.

Relapse prevention groups

Relapse is a devastating event at any stage in a patient's recovery and, since it is always avoidable, every effort is made to prepare patients for the early signs of relapse and to equip them with appropriate preventative strategies. Some advice is practical and generic – for example, reinforcing the benefit of joining an anonymous fellowship and gaining a sponsor. Other aspects of relapse prevention are specific to the individual – for example, identifying patterns of thinking and behaviour that have led to using in the past and will, predictably enough, do the same in the future. Relapse is sometimes regarded as a process rather than an event. In other words, a person is said to be in relapse if they stop engaging with pro-recovery activities such as mixing with people or doing positive behaviours such as exercise or work. At this point, picking up a drink or drug is not yet inevitable but the likelihood is increasing. For this reason, relapse prevention is sometimes known as promoting or enhancing recovery (Coates, 2006).

Offending behaviour group

Problematic substance misuse and criminal activity are intimately linked. This is unsurprising given that the average weekly spend on heroin and crack cocaine is thought to be upwards of £290 per week (NCCMH, 2008). One in a hundred of the general population is thought to use crack cocaine or heroin, while one person in eight who is arrested for acquisitive crime is found to be using these substances (UKDPC, 2008). For them, recovery also means abstaining from all criminal behaviour because resuming offending is commonly linked to a return to using. Offending behaviour groups provide the scope for individuals to discuss their behaviour in a safe, supportive environment and to role play and practise scenarios in which they may be tempted to resort to 'old behaviour'. The format for such programmes varies greatly and, while 'problem-solving' approaches have indicated some positive results, the overall evidence base is currently weak (UKDPC, 2008).

Case study 5.3   Howard

Howard is in extended care having completed his detox and primary treatment. He is now able to travel to the local town unsupervised. Staff members have been pleased with his progress. However, the mood in the community is unsettled amid rumours that drugs are about to be supplied. Howard's name comes up as it emerges that he has been selling items of fashion clothing to other patients. The multidisciplinary team is aware that Howard has little available cash to have purchased these items. Howard appears generally withdrawn and becomes evasive when his counsellor asks him about the clothes.

Gender group

In mixed-sex establishments, gender groups allow men and women to attend a therapy group with members of their own sex providing the opportunity to discuss issues that might be hard to introduce to a mixed-sex environment. Gender groups can be highly off-putting to participants and are often unpopular. Substance misuse has a strong correlation with high-risk sexual behaviour – 48 per cent of service users admit to having had unprotected sex, with 26 per cent of these volunteering that this activity was not with their regular partner (Jones et al., 2007). Group participants may experience high levels of shame associated with this and a large group of males can be seen as a greater source of judgement and criticism than a mixed group.

REFLECTION POINT

Facilitating therapy groups is part of the work of the counsellor in a residential setting.

- Would you welcome or feel daunted by this aspect of the work?
- Might you need further training?

Alternative therapies

Evidence is gathering for the effectiveness of some alternative therapies in the treatment of addiction (Prentiss, 2006). While reiki or acupuncture might or might not act directly on the addictive process, they certainly provide patients with an alternative means of achieving relaxation and relief from stress that does not involve substances (Margolin et al., 2002).

Leisure activities

Most treatment centres have a variety of in-house activities as well as some provided outside of the centre itself. These may include trips out, walking, shopping, cinema, bowling or special events like a meal out. They not only provide light and shade to the general stress of treatment, but also provide patients with an experience of 'living normally' without the use of substances.

Therapeutic duties

Therapeutic duties include day-to-day tasks that aid the running and upkeep of the treatment centre. These will include cleaning and tidying bedrooms, communal areas and maybe some kitchen duties. Some of the early rehabilitation centres used 'therapeutic duties' as a form of punishment to aid behaviour modification. Interventions such as punishing 'old behaviour' with back-breaking tasks is now, thankfully, frowned upon. Nevertheless, therapeutic duty is usually unpopular with service users and can be a source of conflict when certain individuals are considered not to be pulling their weight. The positive benefit of such duties, however, is the restoration of personal pride. When patients reflect on their ability to maintain both themselves and their immediate environment, they are able to recognise a positive, growthful aspect of themselves that they may have long since forgotten. The effect is very motivating.

REFLECTION POINT

Consider your training and experience to date.

- What are your strengths in the light of the interventions listed above?
- Where are there shortfalls in your experience and skills?
- How might you have managed some of the scenarios described above?
- What issues might you need to consider with regard to risk that differ from other workplaces?

Working with substance misusers

- The therapist must provide consistent and clear boundaries by maintaining standards of conduct for themselves and patients, including intervention start and end times, dress standards and group format.
- The therapist is frequently viewed as a positive role model and will be greeted enthusiastically if he or she is able to communicate the joy of substance-free living, though they may also be viewed with suspicion and distrust, and may be 'tested' by individuals in treatment to confirm a negative, hopeless or distrustful view of the world.
- Confidence and spontaneity are helpful in converting conflict and resistance into learning and growth.

THE TWELVE-STEP PROGRAMME OF ALCOHOLICS ANONYMOUS

The twelve-step programme forms the basis of therapeutic treatment programmes in many residential treatment centres and some knowledge of the approach is essential for any therapist working in the field, whether or not they intend to incorporate it into their practice.

The twelve-step programme is synonymous with Alcoholics Anonymous and all of the other 'anonymous' groups, which are also known as 'fellowships' and meet in all major towns and cities (and many smaller ones too) worldwide, providing a free network of support to active or recovering addicts. Some individuals have achieved 'sobriety' using the fellowship alone, some receive treatment first and then progress to the fellowship as a bridge between treatment and 'normality' while others fully embrace their groups and attend regularly for decades. Both the fellowship and the programme espouse very clear principles.

- Addiction is a disease of the mind and body which is progressive by nature and for which there is no known cure.
- One can achieve remission from the disease if abstinent and working the twelve-step programme.

For a clear description of the inception of Alcoholics Anonymous, there is no better starting point than the eponymous Alcoholics Anonymous standard text. The twelve steps can be found in Table 5.2.

Where the twelve-step programme is integrated into a treatment centre's philosophy, it is common that only the first three of four steps are completed during primary treatment. The full twelve-step programme is usually

---

1. We admitted we were powerless over alcohol, that our lives had become unmanageable.
2. Came to believe that a Power greater than ourselves could restore us to sanity.
3. Made a decision to turn our will and our lives over to the care of God as we understood Him.
4. Made a searching and fearless moral inventory of ourselves.
5. Admitted to God, to ourselves and to another human being the exact nature of our wrongs.
6. Were entirely ready to have God remove all these defects of character.
7. Humbly asked Him to remove our shortcomings.
8. Made a list of all persons we had harmed, and became willing to make amends to them all.
9. Made direct amends to such people wherever possible, except when to do so would injure them or others.
10. Continued to take personal inventory and when we were wrong promptly admitted it.
11. Sought through prayer and meditation to improve our conscious contact with God as we understood Him, praying only for knowledge of His will for us and the power to carry that out.
12. Having had a spiritual awakening as the result of these steps, we tried to carry this message to alcoholics and to practise these principles in all our affairs.

(Alcoholics Anonymous, 2001, p59)

Table 5.2: Alcoholics Anonymous twelve-step programme.

worked with the assistance of a sponsor over a period of months or years. The first three steps form a unit that has been described as *I can't. He can. Let him.* In taking the first step, participants accept that alcohol has come to control them. In the face of this powerlessness, the second step invites participants to identify and experience a greater power that will support them. During step three, participants make a decision to live their lives according to God (the power identified in step 2) and, in so doing, give up on their own destructive 'self-will' which has lead them into alcoholism. Step four is the start of a new phase in the programme where, now 'sober', participants begin the process of embracing a new, spiritual approach to life by honestly identifying their 'defects of character'.

REFLECTION POINT

- How does your theoretical orientation relate to the twelve-step programme, in particular the concepts of 'powerlessness' and 'defects of character'?
- What do you think will be the greatest personal challenges to you of working with this approach?
- How do you view the role of spirituality within therapy?

CHALLENGES TO THE PATIENT AND THERAPIST

Addiction treatment is rarely a smooth ride. At any given moment in a treatment centre, one or more patients will be encountering a crisis point. It is so normal for treatment to be punctuated with such difficulties that a smooth ride through residential treatment is often regarded with suspicion. Potential flashpoints in treatment are described below.

The 'rattle'

Patients who are undergoing detoxification will be given a rapidly reducing dose of their substitute drug. Alcohol detoxification is usually achieved with a long-acting benzodiazepine like diazepam and is usually a painless experience. Reducing doses of benzodiazepine are also employed for individuals who have been abusing 'benzos'. In such cases, the individual may encounter very troubling psychological and/or emotional symptoms, even if the physical detoxification is straightforward. Examples of these include high levels of anxiety or paranoia (National Collaborating Centre for Mental Health, 2008). For opiate users, a reducing dose of a heroin substitute such as methadone is used. In these instances, patients are highly likely to experience unpleasant physical withdrawals as well as psychological disturbance. Since shakes or tremors often accompany withdrawals, this stage is colloquially known as a 'rattle'.

It is common for patients to decide to leave during their withdrawals. Therapists, nurses and support workers will rally the client's peers to encourage the individual to stay and they may well spend a good deal of time listening, cajoling, persuading and encouraging. Sometimes, such interventions help the patient see out their detox. Sadly, however, patients may well leave treatment in varying degrees of haste.

Even after the withdrawal, patients may elect to leave treatment before their care plan has been achieved. Reasons for leaving are many and varied but they are frequently linked to the re-experiencing of difficult emotions at a time when they are without their usual coping strategy. For the therapist, it can be hard to distinguish between 'reasons' and 'excuses' for leaving treatment. Equally, patients may be unable to distinguish the real reason for leaving.

Case study 5.4   Susan

Susan had a difficult time detoxing from heroin. However, once through her withdrawals, Susan began to enjoy life in the treatment centre and quickly established friendships with both male and female peers. Further into her treatment, Susan began spending time speaking to old friends on the phone and became isolated as her mood lowered. Finding the sheen on her recovery fading, Susan lost hope in a brighter future and returned to old relationships for familiarity. During a weekend visit from a 'family member' Susan simply left treatment with just a few belongings thrown into a bin liner.

Addiction to substances is just one part of a complex set of circumstances and factors for the addict. For some, real, tangible changes in behaviour and lifestyle are not a priority once apparent 'sobriety' has been achieved. The bio-psycho-social model of addiction provides a framework for understanding the complex nature of addiction (Donovan and Marlatt, 1988).

Relationships

Some practitioners have suggested that attachment problems or relational difficulties lie at the heart of all addiction problems (Whitfield, 1987; Schaeffer, 1987). Indeed, substance misuse is sometimes referred to as a 'chemical relationship'. The phenomenon of sudden and often explosive 'love' relationships in treatment seems to support this theory, at least in part. Where treatment centres are mixed sex, even the most unlikely of relationships can be formed. Relationships and 'sexual politics' can disturb the atmosphere in a treatment centre. For the individuals concerned, their treatment is severely threatened since they may lose interest in recovery and gain a false sense of euphoria. When the relationship ends, however, the individuals are frequently left emotionally shattered and at risk of relapsing. Some treatment centres avoid these problems by operating a single sex service, limiting the scope for relationship difficulties.

Attempting to engage therapeutically with a patient who has exchanged drug addiction for a relationship is extremely challenging and can leave the therapist feeling deeply unskilled. Furthermore, attempts to 'persuade' a patient to stay in treatment are frequently met with equal and opposite justification to leave. The therapist is well advised to resist such efforts and, instead, advise their client to seek a range of views from peers and staff.

Being 'pulled out' of treatment

While patients are in treatment, they often leave family members or significant people behind. This is often a cause of acute stress for the patient who may feel that they are letting down their family or, in the first flush of sobriety, feel a desperate hurry to make amends for their behaviour during active addiction. Alternatively, patients may want to maintain contact with a significant other who may not be helpful to them. Such instances may include destructive or abusive relationships or a relationship in which the person out of treatment continues to misuse substances.

Case study 5.5   Harry

Harry is in his mid-fifties and suffers from alcoholism. He is very remorseful about his drinking, having entered treatment following the breakdown of his marriage and has engaged well with the programme. Harry has described his heartache at the strain he has put on his wife. However, it becomes increasingly apparent in individual therapy that the relationship is founded on Harry taking responsibility for his wife's well-being as she suffers from anxiety and social phobia while she continues to 'support' him with his problems. Harry feels a weight of responsibility for his wife but also feels that he has let her down. Harry advises you that he has spoken to his wife and she is ready to have him back. He is leaving treatment tomorrow.

REFLECTION POINT

Reflect on your experience of working with co-dependency.

- What might Harry be experiencing in his relationship that is related to his drinking?
- How would you engage with Harry so that he might think through his decision?

Relapse

Many centres insist that relapse, though unfortunate for the individual concerned, must result in the termination of treatment. This policy keeps the treatment centre 'safe', as illicit substances will, by and large, be kept out of the premises. Other centres take a view that relapse is a predictable part of the process and endeavour to help the individual understand their relapse, learn from it and move forward. Relapse is a devastating setback for the individual concerned, especially if they had a genuine desire to remain abstinent. However, the treatment centre must tread a fine line between understanding and supporting the individual and inadvertently promoting a policy of permissiveness. Either way, relapse is damaging for the patient and can be harmful to the stability and well-being of the entire community. Referring agencies, e.g. Drug Action Teams or the Probation Service, will require information on the relapse. This information will play a part in their decision to continue funding treatment or not.

SELF-CARE

As a therapist in a treatment centre, it can be very hard to watch your efforts apparently going to waste in the face of any, or all, of the challenges described above. Huge efforts go into persuading patients to remain in treatment rather than watch them give up at a critical time. The effect is particularly wearying, especially when you are faced with several conflicting demands simultaneously. It is often the case that, when one person leaves treatment, others follow (as the obsession with the inevitable substance use grows). At the same time as persuading a patient to remain in treatment, you may be liaising with a nurse to obtain essential medication and providing harm minimisation advice to the patient and family members. Additionally, you may be liaising with the referring organisation to help ensure that community assistance is provided and speaking with the Probation Service if the person is facing being 'breached'.

A 'normal' day may be no less tiring. In a typical healthcare setting, shifts are up to 12 hours long with employees working 'day on – day off'. A typical shift might include standard duties of:

- two community meetings;
- two group therapy sessions;
- team handovers;
- a series of one-to-one sessions;
- writing up multidisciplinary team notes, writing progress reports to funding bodies, completing TOP forms (Treatment Outcome Profiles – a tool for substance misuse professionals to monitor the outcomes of treatment, including data on substance use, injecting behaviour, crime, and health and social functioning);

- providing phone or written updates to funding organisations or referrers.

In addition, the therapist will attend to a constant flow of queries and requests from patients who look to you for advice, information and help with issues inside and out of treatment. You may be asked to intervene in disputes between patients or to provide special dispensation to miss a group or activity for any number of reasons. The demand for your services will be constant and may vary from advice regarding whether or not to speak to police officers about abuse experienced in childhood to a request to fix a leaking tap. Both individuals may regard their request as your top priority!

As a therapist in a residential treatment setting, you are part of the everyday 'furniture' for patients. You must adhere to the 'rules' of the establishment and you must play your part in maintaining them. The stress experienced by patients can rub off onto staff. Patients may try to manipulate you by any number of methods in order to achieve their aims. They may pass responsibility for their well-being to you and they may blame you if they are unhappy. They may disagree with your decisions and your interventions and may complain that you are not helping them. They may even blame you for relapsing or their decision to leave treatment.

In group and individual interventions, patients will make disclosures that may be shocking. Containing distress in groups can be challenging. Your capacity to remain present to another person's suffering may not be mirrored by other members of the group who may want to leave or blame you for their peer's distress. On other occasions it may be difficult to contain your own distress. While it may pay to remain stoical in a group, it is essential that your feelings find expression somewhere. Given the extent of distressing material disclosed and the volume of groups delivered, both compassion fatigue and desensitisation remain an ever-present threat to the therapist (US Department of Health and Human Services, 2005).

In spite of the many and varied challenges to the therapist, working in a treatment centre can become captivating and preoccupying. It can be very hard to leave work at the allotted time if issues are left unresolved. It is equally easy to continue engaging mentally with clients beyond the end of the working day. Remembering the simple maxim that the therapist should not have to consistently work harder than the client is very apt in this field. There are plenty of opportunities to 'go beyond the call of duty'. However, the opportunities to sit back and recharge are very few and far between.

ACTIVITY 5.3

Reflect on your mechanisms for self-care.

- Beyond your supervision arrangements, make a list of things you are currently doing to maintain your own emotional and physical (and spiritual) well-being.

PROFESSION STRUCTURE AND CONTINUING PROFESSIONAL DEVELOPMENT

It is estimated that currently around 30,000 people work in the field of substance misuse in the UK, with counselling being one specific profession within the field (**www.fdap.org.uk/careers/careers**.html). Some counsellors (like me) qualify in general counselling (with a diploma level qualification recognised by BACP or one of the other main accrediting bodies in the UK). Others become formally qualified as addictions counsellors through courses recognised by the Federation of Drug and Alcohol Professionals (FDAP). Clearly, such a qualification is a major advantage in acquiring this type of work.

While such courses offer a complete training in their own right, they inevitably limit the newly qualified trainee to the drug and alcohol field. Similarly, a newly qualified counsellor with a 'general' qualification might find it hard to break into the drug and alcohol field without additional experience or learning. Helpful solutions to this problem might include volunteering with local drug and alcohol projects (these might involve informal counselling in community settings, e.g. youth clubs) or undertaking short relevant training in the field. DAATs commission such services and will be able to provide information on both. Some DAATs offer online training and even free face-to-face training events that provide the opportunity to learn about the field as well as meet relevant local service providers.

I would recommend that newly qualified counsellors seek as wide a variety of additional voluntary experience as possible. I strengthened my application for work in a residential treatment centre, having focused my MA dissertation on the subject of addiction. However, my previous voluntary experience assisting a local men's group as well as work in a previous and apparently unrelated career proved to be invaluable both at interview and in the role itself.

Many treatment centres employ staff who would describe themselves as 'in recovery' or as 'former addicts'. Patients in treatment centres can feel very reassured in being assigned to a counsellor who has inside knowledge and who is not a 'textbook' counsellor. It is also exceptionally helpful for patients to have living, breathing examples of the rewards of sticking to the programme! Treatment centres frequently have a policy of employing recovering addicts after they have been clean for a substantial length of time – e.g. two years. They may join as a general support worker (paid or voluntary) and receive on-the-job training as well as encouragement in attending professional training. It is also possible for people without previous personal experience of drug addiction to enter the field this way, though it is much less common and will almost certainly entail a period of voluntary work.

CHAPTER SUMMARY

Residential drug and alcohol treatment differs significantly from conventional therapy in its requirement for directivity, the sharing of confidentiality and the work of the therapist being just one aspect of the patient's treatment plan.

It is a demanding and frequently draining job and the therapist must tread a fine line between potential burn-out on the one hand and compassion-fatigue and desensitisation on the other.

Opportunities for feeling deskilled are ever present and the therapist must ensure that they are well supported by colleagues and their supervisor as well as providing adequate mechanisms for self-care.

Addictions treatment remains statistically an uphill battle and it is essential that the therapist does not get hooked on success.

At the same time, residential addictions therapy remains a captivating and highly rewarding endeavour with the opportunity to witness and contribute to some outstanding examples of human transformation.

SUGGESTED FURTHER READING

Alcoholics Anonymous (2001) *Alcoholics Anonymous* 4th edition. New York: Alcoholics Anonymous World Services.

Gorski, T (1991) *Understanding the Twelve Steps*. New Jersey: Prentice Hall.

Two useful texts giving insight into the twelve-step approach.

Frey, J (2004) *A Million Little Pieces*. London: Hodder Headline.

Nakken, C (1990) *The Addictive Personality: Understanding the addictive process and compulsive behavior*. Minnesota: Hazelden Information and Educational Services.

Useful for broadening one's understanding of addiction in general.

Peterson, T and McBride, A (2002) *Working with Substance Misusers.* London: Routledge.

Provides useful information on multidisciplinary treatment of addiction, assessment and care planning.

Prentiss, C (2006) *The Alcoholism and Addiction Cure – A holistic approach to total recovery.* Los Angeles, CA: Power Press.

These texts give an idea of treatment from the service user's perspective.

ONLINE RESOURCES

www.castlecraig.co.uk/patients_and_families/treatment_programme/ complementary_ therapies/art_therapy.aspx Castle Craig Hospital – examples of art created by patients.

www.nta.nhs.uk National Treatment Association – provides up-to-date information on government policy in the UK.

www.rcpsych.ac.uk Royal College of Psychiatrists – provides useful information from a medical perspective.

CHAPTER 6

Counselling and psychotherapy in prisons

Norman Claringbull

CORE KNOWLEDGE

- Devoting therapeutic resources to prisoner welfare schemes aimed at reducing offending behaviour can often be beneficial to both inmates and society.
- Significant mental health issues appear to affect at least 50 per cent of all prison inmates.
- The incidence of alcohol and drugs misuse problems among all offenders is exceptionally high and studies typically suggest that such concerns affect at least 65 per cent of all offenders (prisoners and arrestees).
- Prison lifestyles and prison regimes have a significant impact on choices of counselling and psychotherapeutic methodologies.
- The transitory and disruptive nature of routine prison life suggests that the shorter-term, high-impact, therapies are more likely to be useful treatment methods than the longer-term therapies.
- Establishing productive client/therapist working alliances is particularly difficult in prison settings, so therapists need to pay careful attention to planning treatment strategies.
- Prisoner-clients often have complex needs. Therefore, prison-based counsellors and psychotherapists need to be very flexible and innovative in their therapeutic approaches.
- Prisoner-clients are often vulnerable and at risk of suicide, self-harm or harm from others. Counsellors and psychotherapists will need specific training in working with risk and to be familiar with the policies and referral routes of the particular institution(s) in which they work.
- Counselling and psychotherapy are more likely to benefit inmates and to more productively use therapists' skills if they are delivered as part of overall prisoner care and management. They often need to be provided as integral elements in multidisciplinary welfare packages.

INTRODUCTION

In this chapter you will be introduced to the role played by counsellors and psychotherapists in prisons, to the history of psychological interventions in the penal system, and to current debates about the place of counselling and psychotherapy in prisons today.

You will be asked to think beyond the usual confines of the counselling room to consider the implications of counselling in the context of a publicly funded system that has limited funds to service the needs of competing priorities and stakeholders.

You will also be given an insight into the day-to-day challenges and rewards of working in a stressful and challenging environment with some of the most deprived, isolated and demonised individuals in our society.

HISTORICAL PERSPECTIVES

The place of counselling and psychotherapy in prisons might not be as new a development as some modern practitioners might suppose. After all, encouraging actual or potential offenders to reform their supposedly incorrect ways of behaving, or at least persuading or compelling them to conform to society's norms, has long been an objective for many criminal justice and social punishment systems. In that sense, applying psychological pressures or treatments aimed at 'officially approved' attitude changes is in no way a modern concept.

Throughout the history of incarceration, as it has existed in many human societies, the intentions of those in power have been clear – to punish the guilty and to protect themselves and their societies. Sometimes they have even tried to bring wrongdoers to some form of socially acceptable salvation (Morris and Rothman, 1995). However, the reality on the ground has been that all too often prisons have actually been institutions of social control and bases for individual and society-wide oppression (Johnston, 2008). This has meant that throughout the ages, more often than not, prisons have been little more than inhumane criminal warehouses where despair reigned and hope died. Such dehumanising establishments had little use for counsellors or counselling.

Nevertheless, in some parts of the world, improvements in society's attitudes to prisoners and improvements in prison conditions did begin to slowly emerge. This has especially been the case in some parts of Europe and the United States over the last two to three hundred years. Often, this re-humanising process was due to the efforts of influential prisoner-welfare workers and inmates-rights champions such as Elizabeth Fry (1780–1845;

UK) or Dorothea Dix (1802–87; US). Prominent among the prison reformers in the UK was the founding father of humane penal policies, John Howard (1726–90), from whom the modern Howard League for Prison Reform takes its name. Campaigners such as these were concerned with promoting the transformation of the offender through the supposed beneficial influence of humane prison conditions. Today, as counsellors and psychotherapists, we might almost see some aspects of those sorts of correctional policies as being akin to early forms of psychological therapy.

Some of the earliest appearances of psychological therapies in prisons came about because of the notion held in some quarters in the early to mid-twentieth century that the ideal reforming prison would be based on the principles of a psychotherapeutic community (Rotman, 1995). In this model of penal policy, the 'bad' prisoner becomes the 'maladjusted' prisoner and so 'criminal' means 'sick'. It remains the case that this emphasis on promoting the psychological and emotional health of offenders seems to be a core factor (or at least a core intention) in much of modern prisoner management. Of course, the meaning of the term 'emotional good health' in this context is a debatable topic.

Reforming the offender is supposedly one of the core purposes of modern-day prison policy in the UK. For example, on its 2010 website, the UK Prison Service declares that its primary purpose includes:

> *Her Majesty's Prison Service serves the public by keeping in custody those committed by the courts. Our duty is to look after them with humanity and help them lead law-abiding and useful lives in custody and after release.*
>
> **(www.hmprisonservice.gov.uk/aboutthe service/statementofpurpose)**

It could be argued that the sorts of individual offender reform that these apparently beneficent intentions clearly demand have links to the sorts of personal reforms that are of interest to counsellors, to psychotherapists, and to their clients. Examples of such areas of potential psychological growth could include improved self-knowledge and self-awareness, appropriate behaviour modifications and so on.

REFLECTION POINT

- 'Cure', 'change' or 'help' – what should prison counsellors focus on?
- Are some offenders 'beyond' psychotherapy?
- What do you think are the key tasks of prison counsellors and psychotherapists?

CURRENT TRENDS

In 2007, the UK prison authorities produced a thematic review of the needs of and available support for prisoners with mental/emotional health needs (Lloyd et al., 2007). This review began by citing an original core position statement from the then Chief Inspector of Prisons:

> *There is particularly urgent need for increased provision for the care of those with mental health problems, who make up a larger proportion of the prison population than they would of any other group in the community. What is more, prison can exacerbate mental health problems, which has a long-term impact on the individual concerned and the community into which he or she may be released.*
>
> (HM Chief Inspector of Prisons, 2002,
> cited in Lloyd et al., 2007, p5)

It also cited a statement from the 2002 Director-General of the Prison Service:

> *Since the late 1980s the proportion of the prison population who show signs of mental illness has risen seven-fold. For them, care in the community has become care in custody [. . .] But I do have what I see as the cavalry coming over the hill in the form of 300 psychiatric nurses from the NHS coming into prison hospitals to offer in-reach services to those who are ill. But the problem is near overwhelming.*
>
> (Director-General of the Prison Service,
> at the British Institute of Human Rights, 2002)

Of course, what is not clear from the Director-General's statement is whether there really has been a genuine increase in the proportion of the prison population with mental health problems. It might simply be that this apparent increase is due to better initial assessment. The strong probability is that the clinically-in-need proportion of the inmate population was always large but it was hidden by ineffective mental health screening. In any event, the known current proportion of prisoners with mental and emotional health problems is huge. This is especially so if alcohol and drug dependency/misuse are included as being diagnosable conditions.

Lloyd et al. (2007) reported that, by 2002, responsibility for the mental health of prisoners had passed from the Prison Service to the National Health Service and that by 2006 some 80 per cent of all prisons apparently had nurse-led Mental Health In-Reach Teams in place. These teams consisted mainly of psychiatric nurses who had various levels of access to psychiatrists, clinical psychologists, occupational therapists, drugs workers and counsellors. In addition, Counselling, Assessment, Referral, Advice and Throughcare (CARAT) workers are now in place in most prisons to help inmates with alcohol and substance misuse problems.

All of the recent studies of prison populations have found that there is an enormous level of mental health need among the inmates. For example, Lloyd et al. (2007) suggest that:

- 50 per cent of all prisoners have primary or secondary mental health needs;
- 45 per cent of all prisoners have alcohol or drug misuse problems;
- 17 per cent of all prisoners have a psychiatric history.

They also found that of those inmates who are referred to their prison's Mental Health In-Reach Team:

- 50 per cent suffered from depression and self-harming behaviour;
- 70 per cent had substance misuse needs;
- 50 per cent had physical health needs.

It is also very interesting from a counselling point of view to note that when measured by a standard mental health evaluation tool (General Health Questionnaire 12):

- 65 per cent of all female prisoners showed a need for emotional support;
- 52 per cent of all male prisoners showed a need for emotional support;
- 27 per cent of all young prisoners showed a need for emotional support.

The Lloyd et al. (2007) investigations, when added to the many other UK and international studies of prison populations (Stewart, 2008; Useem, 2008) provide overwhelming evidence that there is a huge actual and potential demand from prisoners for help with their emotional and psychological problems. In sum, as the Current Chief Inspector of Prisons says:

> *Those who end up in our prisons have complex and long-standing mental health needs: often linked to substance misuse, and ranging from acute psychosis, through personality disorder, to high levels of anxiety and depression. Some prisoners also, or alternatively, have learning disabilities. And these needs are themselves only part of a more complex picture of multiple disadvantage and social exclusion, which may fall through the net of community health, social care, housing and drugs agencies*
>
> (Owers, 2007, p5)

The latest figures (Home Office, 2007) show that only about 25 per cent of all offenders received an immediate custodial sentence. As noted above, problems of social exclusion and disadvantage often precipitate offending behaviour. The possibility exists, therefore, that in appropriate cases, referral to a specialist counselling and/or psychotherapeutic service might be a substitute for incarceration.

DIVERGENT VIEWS OF COUNSELLING IN PRISONS

Of particular concern to humanistic counsellors is the widespread impression found throughout the Prison Service that person-centred counselling, with its focus on the individual prisoner's difficulties in isolation, is unhelpful. Interestingly, although the HM Prison Inspector's Thematic Review does support a need for counselling and psychotherapy in prisons, it only does so on the grounds that such therapeutic inputs should be targeted and specialised. General purpose, vaguely-targeted, self-exploratory counselling was not seen as likely to be particularly useful. However, counselling focused on such issues as bereavement, post-traumatic stress, sexual abuse, alcohol/drugs misuse, relationship problems, etc., was considered to be potentially beneficial. The central theme among those interested in rehabilitating inmates seems to be that counselling in prisons should be part of an overall offender care and management package, and not an isolated exercise undertaken for its own (possibly ill-defined) sake. Taken all round, however, it seems that counselling and counsellors do have something to offer prisoners although there is a clear need to more fully investigate just what that role should be (Lloyd et al., 2007).

Table 6.1 summarises two divergent views of the purposes of counselling and psychotherapy in prisons.

REFLECTION POINT

Consider your own therapeutic orientation and training.

- Who in your view is the primary stakeholder/client of counselling and psychotherapy in prisons?
- Do prison counsellors and psychotherapists have a responsibility to the wider society?
- Does holding a supposedly achievable non-judgemental attitude mean that counsellors should adopt a morally neutral attitude towards criminals who engage in socially disruptive behaviour?

Therapeutic aims/ emphasis	• Prisoner reform and rehabilitation • Managing offending behaviour • Developing skills for living • Reducing burden on society • Improving well-being	• Rehabilitation of the person • Managing emotional and psychological disturbance • Self-exploration • Self-development • Managing relationships • Managing destructive behaviours • Improving well-being
Stakeholders/ beneficiaries	Home Office Prison Service Society in general Inmate	Inmate Prison community Society in general
Primary investor	Home Office	Home Office Voluntary organisations
Therapeutic orientation(s)	Behavioural Cognitive Pedagogic Problem specific Goal oriented Short term	Non-directive Non-judgemental Empathic Relational Long and short term

Table 6.1: Divergent views of counselling and psychotherapy in prisons.

THE NEED FOR COUNSELLING IN PRISONS

As we have already noted, there is a significant need among prisoners for the sorts of healthcare that counsellors and psychotherapists can provide. Numerous studies (Brooker et al., 2002; Lloyd et al., 2007; Rickford, 2003; Rickford and Edgar, 2005) have identified the extent of the problem and these studies all lead to the conclusion that there are many ways in which talking therapies can contribute to the overall primary mental healthcare of prison inmates. For example, taken overall, these studies suggest that:

- about 50 per cent of patient-inmates suffer from depression or the need to self-harm and that at least 10 per cent exhibit anxiety symptoms;
- the most common psychotherapeutic interventions available to these sufferers include CBT (about 60 per cent) and counselling (35–40 per cent).

Lloyd et al.'s (2007) enquiries also support the belief that many Prison Service GPs strongly support the need for more access to the talking therapies to be made available to such prisoners. Their study also argues that there is an obvious need to support the encouragement of emotional well-being among inmates. However, they also found that only 24 per cent of prison Mental Health In-Reach Teams believed that they had sufficient resources to meet the needs of inmates.

Lloyd et al. also found that quite a variety of Prisoner Care Programme Approach 'bolt-ons' could sometimes be on offer to the inmates. These included:

- psychosocial interventions;
- occupational therapy;
- anxiety management;
- anger management;
- group work;
- motivational interviewing;
- coping strategy planning;
- health promotion;
- art/dance therapy;
- solution-focused therapy, and so on.

These sorts of activities, all of which fall within the range of services commonly offered by counsellors, were not in practice usually provided by professional counselling practitioners. Often these sorts of therapeutic applications were delivered by other prison workers as adjuncts to their routine duties. Worryingly, Lloyd et al. did not find it possible to determine just how structured and focused these sorts of non-professional applications of counselling and psychological therapies were in terms of how they met the perceived needs of the prison inmates. Of course, this is an unsurprising finding if, as appears to be the case, these counselling and psychotherapeutic interventions were not being delivered by professional practitioners.

THE PRISON POPULATION AND PRESENTING ISSUES

Unless working in a special prison for a particular category of offenders, counsellors and psychotherapists will come across a wide range of clients from all ages and backgrounds, although the segregation of the sexes in prisons means that counsellors will only work with one sex according to the designation of the prison. However, this does not preclude the issue of working with transgendered people or inmates who are transitioning.

Fred Linsell (an independent prisons counsellor) writes:

> *The prison inmates that I have met are a very mixed bunch. They have included a cross-section of many cultural, religious, social and sexual backgrounds. Young Offenders Institutes where I have worked cover ages*

from 16 to 21 years old. Their adult counterparts have inmates ranging from 21 years old onwards and this has included in some cases inmates approaching their seventies. The crimes committed by these prisoners came from right across the board. These included anything from non-payment of fines, burglary, drug offences through to rape, paedophilia, arson, and even murder. My experiences came from working with prisoners from all these sorts of backgrounds.

In my opinion, the prison environment is an unnatural one. All of my counselling work was carried out in male prisons. In such locations, a small number of female officers and some limited clerical staff were usually the only females on the prison 'campus'. Where I worked the obvious exception to that situation came from the existence of our small group of female volunteer counsellors. This creates an environment whereby some of the men, although not homosexual, have sought same-sex contact due to having no female counterpart. This was not always for sexual gratification. Often it was simply a means of experiencing close contact with another human being. Therefore, within the counselling sessions, some inmates tentatively approached the fact that they thought they might be gay due to engaging in same-sex relationships. On exploring these feelings, it became apparent to me that the purpose of these relationships was to provide a level of comfort to both parties, one that was missing from their everyday prison lives. Sexuality is a big issue for prisoners.

On the issue of presenting problems, Linsell writes:

Quite often counsellors ask me about what sorts of emotional and psychological problems therapists might find trouble prison inmates. Of course, the list is varied and the real answer is 'anything at all'. However, in my personal experience the 'typical' prisoner problems that counsellors might find themselves having to deal with are:

- *difficult family ties;*
- *death of a spouse, child or family member;*
- *revisiting past problems;*
- *relationship problems, both inside prison and outside family members;*
- *bullying;*
- *access to health facilities and medication;*
- *health problems;*
- *long-term sentences and resultant institutionalisation;*
- *black magic (practised by some inmates upon other inmates);*
- *violence;*
- *childhood, physical, mental and sexual abuse;*
- *educational impoverishment often resulting from poor schooling;*
- *reconnecting with society;*
- *mental health issues;*
- *accommodation on release;*

- *assessment to qualify for release;*
- *risk of suicide;*
- *self-harm;*
- *racism;*
- *finding ways to cope with imprisonment;*
- *employment within prison;*
- *decisions on distance learning and subsequent qualifications;*
- *wanting to learn relaxation techniques.*

ACTIVITY 6.1

Consider the list of presenting problems above. List the issues specific to the prison environment.

- About which issues do you require further information and training?
- How would you set about finding this information?
- Can you think of any other issues specific to imprisonment which may affect your clients?
- What factors might influence the way in which those issues are managed in counselling?

COUNSELLING STYLES

Most practitioners would see counselling and psychotherapy as being usually targeted at helping the individual and often encompassing a wide variety of techniques (Claringbull, 2010; Nelson-Jones, 2002). However, in terms of prison therapy some methods may well prove to be more effective than others, at least in terms of that which is achievable under the particular circumstance of the penal context.

It seems reasonable to suppose that the structure and ethos of a prison as an institution will affect the ways in which counsellors and psychotherapists can relate to their clients. In other words, the styles of counselling that can be adopted are likely to be as much dictated by the realities of prison life as they are by individual prisoner needs. For example, many prisoners either serve very short sentences or are subject to irregular availability due to the uncertainties of the prison regime. These sorts of time constraints would certainly suggest that the shorter-term therapies (e.g. brief-intervention, solution-focused, motivational interviewing, cognitive-behavioural) might be more useful than the longer-term processes such as psychodynamic interventions or some of the humanistic approaches. The irony is that, although prison inmates might be said to have no other real occupation but 'doing time', they still might not have enough time for their therapists.

Therapists need to bear in mind the many studies (e.g. Towl and Crighton, 2002) that indicate that a large number of prisoners have backgrounds that include environmental defects, attachment disorders and addictions. They are also at particular risk of suicide, particularly during the early stages of their incarceration (Towl et al., 2002). These factors all clearly influence decisions about selecting a suitable treatment type. In addition, in some secure settings it would be naive of the therapist to ignore questions of personal safety. Indeed, some crimes might be of a degree or an intensity such as to make it very difficult for the therapist to see the person behind the crime. All of these factors make holding on to a non-judgemental and empathetic humanistic attitude very difficult for many therapists. Clearly, some prisoners will pose a significant threat to the emotional integrity of their therapists. Therefore, counsellors and psychotherapists working in prison settings will need to ensure that they have very robust, very frequent and easily available, clinical supervision arrangements firmly in place.

Practitioner reflections: Power imbalance and the challenge of relating

By Lucy Allison, person-centred counsellor

My first session with a particular client left me feeling overwhelmed with a mixture of emotions from sadness and loss to anger and frustration. It became apparent that supervision was going to be vital for enabling me as the counsellor to work through indisputable reactions and judgements with regard to the person sitting opposite me. There is undoubtedly a sense of imbalance between the client and the counsellor, after all, one of them is holding the keys to leave after the session and so it felt important to be aware of this and to try to distribute the balance as much as possible. The issue around equality in more traditional counselling settings is inevitable but within the prison setting it is even more present. The client shared with me in the second session his discomfort around being told when the session would end; he didn't want to go too deep into his feelings when there was not enough time to slowly close them up again and he felt that I had the power to control this. It was then I realised my mistake, being in a strange room and feeling unfamiliar with the furniture had made me just accept that things stayed where they were, and so, I got up and moved the clock telling him that it was now both our responsibility to be aware of the time we had together and just slightly shifting that power back to him which he then appreciated.

I felt there to be a block between me and this particular client for a couple of sessions and I spent a lot of time in supervision working out my feelings for and around him, one minute I would be feeling all his pain and suffering and then the next he would talk of things that felt so wrong in my eyes, and I would be taken right back to this place of questioning 'how do I really feel about this client?' It was through supervision that I was able to explore that maybe on some levels there were going to be parts of him that I didn't agree with and maybe at times disliked, but there was also another part of him that was vulnerable and confused, and asking myself: 'what does that part of him really need right now?'

One week, not long before we were actually due to finish, he confronted me and questioned if I was fully with him. His openness and honesty hit me full frontal and I realised that what he was doing with me within the session was something he was unable to do with anyone else within this institution. He could not trust, he could not confide, he could not even openly say how at that moment in time he was feeling, yet he had been able to do this with me, and it jolted me. I pushed my negative feelings about what he had done aside and instead saw the man sitting in front of me as he was in that moment. For the rest of the session we were closer, the officer sat outside went unnoticed, the fact that people were able to walk past and look in was not registered, and by the end of a particularly deep and emotional session for him, I looked down and realised I was sat on the edge of my seat as was he; and we were closer.

DRUGS AND ALCOHOL

It is not possible to review the psychological needs of prisoners without acknowledging the place that substance misuse has in their lives. The influence of drugs and alcohol on offending behaviour is clear before arrest, during incarceration, and after release (Home Office Statistical Bulletin, 2008). Various studies come up with various figures (e.g. Bennett, 2000). Typically, they suggest that substance misuse affects more than 60–65 per cent of all offenders (prisoners and arrestees). Conventional wisdom argues that drug misuse is mainly associated with property crime and that alcohol misuse is associated with violent crime (Home Office, 2004). Whatever the true figures are, clearly the problem is huge (see review by Holloway and Bennett, 2004). These observations lead to a dilemma for prison counsellors and psychotherapists. Clearly, there is an obvious need for specialist help for substance-dependent prisoners (see the review by O'Looney, 2005). There are many agencies that specialise in providing such assistance, both inside and outside the prisons. Again, it is clear that counsellors and psychotherapists can play a vital role in such rehabilitation teams. However, counselling in such systems is usually part of an overall care package and often delivered by care workers as a subsidiary activity and not as a professional one. A counsellor working in such circumstances will need to have some clear ideas about acceptable professional boundaries and will probably need to be comfortable with cross-disciplinary working. (See Chapter 5 for further insight into working with addictions and the kinds of cross-disciplinary working this area requires.)

It is likely that any prison counsellor or psychotherapist who does not attempt to uncover a client's true relationship with drink or drugs is potentially doing the client a disservice. Moreover, given the easy access that most prisoners have to covert sources of their drugs of choice during their stay in prison, what is the duty of the therapist towards the authorities in reporting (or not) such breaches of prison discipline?

REFLECTION POINT

You meet a prisoner-client for the first time.

- Do you bring up the subject of substance misuse early in your work with this client?

You discover that your client is actively misusing heroin despite being in prison.

- Do you continue with the therapy?
- If you decide to withdraw from working with this client, how would you explain your decision to the authorities?

WORKING WITH CLIENTS AT RISK

Concomitant with high levels of mental distress in the prison population is the perception of high levels of suicide and self-harm. An awareness of risk factors and training in risk assessment is vital for counsellors working with vulnerable inmates. A Working Party Report of the Royal College of Psychiatrists (RCPsych) notes:

> *High-risk factors for suicide among prisoners are similar to those among other citizens, i.e. youth, male gender, depression, alcoholism and loss of a relative, friend or partner. There is some evidence that more supportive prison regimes may experience less suicidal behaviour than less supportive regimes. There is growing belief that self-help among prisoners is particularly important.*
>
> (2002, p5)

Among other recommendations, the RCPsych Report notes that:

> *There is a need for a more appropriate model of mental health care delivery within prisons. There is a need for better screening for suicidal ideas and propensities at reception and for further assessment and treatment.*
>
> (ibid., p8)

The RCPsych Report also recommends that:

> All prison systems should have a suicide prevention programme clearly identified and widely available.
>
> (ibid., p21)

Given the vulnerability of many clients in prisons, counsellors and psychotherapists will need specific training in working with risk and to be familiar with the policies and referral routes of the particular institution(s) in which they work.

In some prisons, voluntary crisis services are available to inmates who can then be referred onwards for counselling. Fred Linsell notes:

> In many prisons, inmates have access to a small group of fellow prisoners trained by the Samaritans who are called 'Listeners'. The 'Listeners' receive limited training and provide other prisoners, who might have problems, with some access to a support system. 'Listeners' work on a rota which meant that inmates could have access to them on a 24/7 basis. They were also available to stay with an inmate in the Suicide Suite until such time as either the inmate in question was stable enough to return to the prison population, or was hospitalised. The 'Listeners' could also refer the inmate concerned on for counselling if the situation seemed to require it. In my opinion the 'Listeners' did an amazing job under the difficult circumstances that they too endured in the prison environment. They were all volunteers and gave their time freely to anyone who needed them.

The issue of not leaving suicidal inmates alone is highlighted by the 2002 RCPsych Working Party Report that notes:

> The best means of managing a prisoner at risk of suicide is the establishment of constructive relationships between staff and inmates, which again requires special training. Prisoners with obvious mental disturbance should not be placed in solitary confinement and should be managed by closer supervision and support instead, combined, if necessary, with medical care and sedation.
>
> (2002, p21)

REFLECTION POINT

- What are the main 'risk factors' for suicide in prisons?
- How might counselling or psychotherapy contribute to the management of prisoners who are suicidal or at risk of serious self-harm?
- What are your own training needs for working with clients at risk?

DIFFICULTIES

The first task of any counsellor or psychotherapist is to generate a good working relationship with their clients. Put simply, the partners in the therapeutic alliance have to come to trust each other. This can be hard to achieve in a prison setting. As Howerton et al. (2007) found, generally speaking, prisoners don't trust the prison medical staff and this includes not asking for help with mental health issues for fear of stigmatisation.

It appears likely that counsellors and psychotherapists too might be viewed with suspicion by the inmate population. After all, as far as prisoners are concerned, counsellors might well be seen as being more allied with the authorities than they are with their prisoner-clients. This is especially so when it is clear that counsellors cannot act in ways that might compromise public protection. As Walsh (1998) tells us, many inmates will view their counsellors as being part of 'Them', the people who deprived the prisoners of their liberty or who might take away their in-prison privileges. Even more, the counsellors might well be perceived as being part of the system whose goodwill might help to restore their liberty or their withdrawn privileges. Therefore, it will clearly be difficult for prisoner-clients to relate honestly with their counsellors or to view them as a genuine source of help and solace. On the other hand, can counsellors relate openly to clients who they might suspect are trying to manipulate them into perhaps supporting parole applications, transfers to prisons with easier regimes, etc.? 'What's the blighter really after?' might very often be the unstated question routinely troubling both the prisoners and their counsellors.

Another difficulty comes from finding a suitable place to conduct the therapy session within the prison setting. As we know, counselling and psychotherapy require discrete and comfortable locations, regular meetings, no interruptions, no other people in earshot and a feeling of safety. A sense of personal security and a workable level of trust between the parties involved are also essential. Above all, counselling requires privacy and that is a very scarce commodity indeed in most secure environments. None of these desirable, essential even, factors are easily found in UK prisons.

Practitioner reflections: Some features of counselling in a prison

By Fred Linsell, independent prisons counsellor

My work as a prisons counsellor has brought its own unique practice problems. During my time working in prisons I have never experienced what I would call a 'typical counselling day'. I have had to adapt accordingly to the various (and frequently varying) situations which have presented themselves. These circumstances can change very quickly, with 'lock-downs' being called at a moment's notice, usually due to an offence being committed by an inmate or group of inmates. In this situation, inmates are confined to their cells and counselling sessions are therefore not possible. Other factors which can disrupt planned sessions are medical appointments outside the prison environment, court appearances, visits from other outside agencies and even release. Clients may be moved at short notice by the prison authorities to an alternate prison, sometimes due to what was seen as 'unacceptable behaviour' by the inmate. They could also be moved to a less secure prison nearing the end of their sentence due to their being deemed less of an escape risk. All these sorts of disruptions are frequent and are inbuilt in prison life. Clearly, such interruptions in the counselling process lead to prematurely terminated counselling sessions and to an obvious lack of opportunities for closure, for both clients and counsellors.

I have found that prison routine can be disrupted or distorted by a number of factors beyond the counsellor's control. For example:

1. In one prison where I worked, the room normally used for counselling was also designated as the 'Suicide Suite' where inmates were housed when suicide was suspected or attempted. Whenever this room was occupied by an inmate who had been assessed as a suicide risk, I would be abruptly relocated to a different room to meet with my client. Unfortunately, in that particular prison, the substitute room was usually in a more isolated part of the prison. Immediately, this threw up concerns about safety. The prison officers told me that they would have liked to have seen more suitable counselling locations being made available. However, at that time it was just not possible.
2. Inmates, unlike those of us on the outside, cannot choose either their counsellors or indeed a specific counselling model. They are simply allocated a counsellor as and when one becomes available. As the waiting list is so long, it may take quite some time before they are successful in gaining counselling.
3. Initial difficulties on encountering new clients included helping them to understand the concept of confidentiality. Their immediate reaction was to think that any information from our sessions together would be reported to the prison authorities. This was a major first hurdle!

The interpersonal counselling relationship, so central in any form of counselling, is inevitably constrained by the fact that prisons are not only institutions in themselves but they are also source of complex institutionalisation (Copeland, 2005). The objects, regimes and policies of the prison are not necessarily compatible with the ethos of psychotherapy. Constraint comes before counselling, security comes before self-actualisation and punishment comes before personal growth. That is the way of the prison world and the workaday prison therapist has to quickly learn that 'what can't be cured must be endured'.

It is not just the prison environment that militates against the formation of successful therapeutic relationships. The life experiences of clients often result in confusion and ignorance about the possibilities of human relating. Clients can find acceptance and valuing unfamiliar, challenging and difficult. A competent practitioner can model such ways of relating to clients while acknowledging the daily challenges posed to this by the person's environment.

Practitioner reflections: Changing the habits of a lifetime

By Lucy Allison, person-centred counsellor

One of my first clients expressed immediate concerns about counselling which he described as being very far away from his way of relating and expressing himself. He had grown up in a family where violence was congratulated by male members and was used as a way of gaining respect and proving yourself. Acknowledging feelings and talking about them was never an option and he described his fears of doing this. It was apparent that it could take time for him to be able to do this with me.

As the sessions continued and he became more accustomed to being heard and valued, he talked of his feelings of shame and guilt and most significantly of never feeling loved or understood, and he cried openly as he talked about his relationship with his family, particularly his mother with whom he longed to be closer. Being heard and understood by someone who wanted to devote time to him allowed him to talk of many painful moments in his childhood that he confessed never being able to express before. It was very moving to be the person allowed to hear such deep and sometimes dark emotions.

He acknowledged his history of reoffending and we looked at his dreams of a future without crime. His negative feelings towards himself stemmed from the knowledge that all significant women in his life were or had been scared or disgusted by him. I shared my honest feelings of not being scared of him and how I could hear where the anger was coming from. There was always a part of me which questioned how, without help outside of the prison, he would cope and how easy would it be for him to follow this dream he talked of. It felt important, however, for him to express his desire for a new way of being and for him to be able to explore this in an environment which was supportive and not dismissive.

He came in to our third session saying how he had thought about and was looking into becoming a 'listener' (designated people that prisoners can talk to) and also shared his pleasure on having backed away from a physical fight on the wing, even though the verbal abuse towards him had now increased as a result. He explained how he had written an emotional letter to his mother telling her how when he was released he wanted to talk things through with her and explain the reasons behind where he was today.

He seemed to embrace being heard and being able to verbalise how he felt. He started to begin to value himself, which was a new concept for him, and, from this, realised that he deserved to make a better life for himself when he left prison.

ACTIVITY 6.2

Think about establishing a working alliance with a prisoner-client. Make a list of the ways in which the prison environment might act against you and work out some strategies to minimise these difficulties.

ETHICAL DILEMMAS

There are a number of ethical and personal issues that all prison counsellors must bear in mind. Most counsellors and psychotherapists employed in prisons will be required to belong to (and be accredited by) a professional body such as the BACP and will, therefore, be bound to an ethical framework for conduct and professional practice. However, counsellors may need to balance ethical guidance for good therapeutic practice with considerations about their own safety and security.

Prison violence can be directed towards counsellors and psychotherapists too. Counsellors working in prison also have to adapt to the rules and policies of the setting. Therefore, it may be necessary to undergo further training in prison protocol, safety procedures and prison regulations. It goes without saying that entering a personal relationship with a client in any setting has significant ethical implications. However, boundaries around physical distance might need to be negotiated in a prison setting according to the rules of the institution. Examples of boundary and confidentiality issues might include:

- rules about physical contact (no touching whatsoever);
- reporting incidents of inmates receiving drugs;
- reporting attempts to go 'over the wall';
- reporting information about certain categories of crime;
- preventing clients from talking about crimes for which they are yet to be tried;
- reporting abuse where the victim comes under the auspices of guidance for the Protection of Vulnerable Adults (POVA);
- whistle blowing.

Clearly, such issues can lead to conflicts with any counsellor's beliefs about confidentiality and hamper the ability to form a trusting working relationship with a client.

Practitioner reflections: An example of an unusual and complex ethical issue

By Fred Linsell, independent prisons counsellor

On one occasion, although I was asked to work with an individual client, in fact two inmates presented themselves as one of them only had limited English. I was told that the client was Chinese and so he had brought another inmate with him as an interpreter. This did not seem to be a very good idea to me, either professionally or ethically. After all, it was always possible that the inmate acting as an interpreter might return to the wing and tell the rest of the prison population what my client and I had talked about. I asked if we could use a professional interpreter. This was agreed. However, I was told later that the interpreter would be just that, simply an interpreter, and not one trained as a counsellor. Clearly, such a person could not be expected to understand confidentiality issues or to appreciate that the sessions might well cover some distressing subjects. I considered the ethical duty I had towards both my client and the interpreter. For example, one worry that I had was the possibility that the possible disclosure of harrowing information might traumatise the interpreter. I therefore decided to decline this case on ethical grounds until a more appropriate interpreter could be organised. Language difficulties are quite common in prison counselling and I have employed art therapy and used drawings to try and help circumvent this barrier. These attempts have often met with positive results.

OTHER APPLICATIONS OF COUNSELLING IN PRISONS

It is generally the case that the prisoner population is often transient whereas the staff population is far less so. Therefore, it might be argued that counsellors would be better employed on teaching/supervising counselling skills to the permanent staff rather than in directly treating the inmates themselves. It is possible that much useful therapeutic work could be carried out as a sort of 'trickle-down effect' from suitably trained and sympathetic members of the permanent staff. Very often, importing outside 'experts' might be less productive or effective. This 'remote control' style of psychotherapy might be especially useful in modern prison regimes where overall 'Offender Care Packages' are (at least in theory) the order of the day. One thing is certain, any counsellor or psychotherapist going into a prison to work with the inmates (or the staff) who has preconceived ideas about what therapy should entail or must entail is in for a rude awakening. Like the talking therapies generally, flexibility is increasingly the name of the game.

ROUTES INTO THE PROFESSION

Increasingly, counselling in prisons is undertaken by specialist providers who hold contracts with local prison authorities. As noted above, there are other services such as the CARAT teams that are provided nationally by HM Prison Service and whose work includes addressing psychological and emotional problems of inmates in the context of other targeted work (e.g. tackling drug addictions and reducing offending behaviour). Entry into the profession of prison counsellor/psychotherapist is likely to be via one of these formal routes. However, experience as a volunteer or in a variety of care-related roles can also be a useful step-up to counselling. Prison counsellors will be expected to meet professional requirements for training and accreditation unless working in a voluntary 'befriending' capacity.

Fred Linsell describes his route into the profession:

> *What now seems to be a very long time ago, I was working for a County Drug and Alcohol Advisory Service (CDAS) as a volunteer 'befriender' to some of their clients who were using the CDAS drop-in facility. Because of the experience that I was gaining in this particular area of what we now call the Talking Therapies, I was asked to help with setting up a Drugs and Alcohol counselling service for the inmates of four prisons located in the county. As part of the development of what was then a new service, (and the development of some new counsellors), I underwent some appropriate training courses. These included my undergoing some advanced training in suitable counselling methods. Since then I have gradually upgraded my counselling qualifications and I am now the proud holder of a counselling honours degree. Over the last 20 years I have continued to work within secure prison environments. Although in my early days in prison alcohol and drugs counselling I was a CDAS worker, I have subsequently moved towards being an independent prisons counsellor and I no longer concern myself solely with drugs and alcohol misuse issues.*

CHAPTER SUMMARY

Working in a prison is perhaps one of the most challenging endeavours for any counsellor or psychotherapist. Many things militate against successful outcomes for counselling in prisons. The physical environment, which by its very nature seems diametrically opposed to the notions of trust, acceptance and empathy central to any counselling interaction, forms a backdrop to the challenges of attitude, policy and client group that counsellors and psychotherapists have to overcome in this line of work. In addition, counsellors and psychotherapists have to negotiate many ethical hurdles, in particular in relation to boundaries, confidentiality and establishing trust.

Counsellors and psychotherapists may also be faced with vulnerable and sometimes debased individuals who by their very status as prisoners have not only been deemed a risk to society but who may well pose a serious risk to themselves. However, as the chapter shows, counsellors and psychotherapists can do valuable work with prisoners and staff members alike. There is some evidence that structured short-term work within the context of a multi-disciplinary package of prisoner reform can benefit prisoners and subsequently society in general. The qualities of the therapist in establishing trust and a strong working alliance are foremost in this kind of work and humanistic therapies can offer ways of relating that many prisoners may never have experienced before. Working in prisons requires a kind of fearlessness and belief in the value of the work itself that, in the face of such contextual difficulties, many counsellors might find hard to sustain. However, for those who enter this line of work, the contextual difficulties can be overcome by hard work and resilience underlined by a commitment to the dignity and humanity of their clients.

SUGGESTED FURTHER READING

Hanser, D, Scott, M and Braddock, A (2010) *Correctional Counseling.* New Jersey: Prentice-Hall.

An American book but still applicable to UK situations. Very much a hands-on book written by real-life practitioners.

Harvey, J and Smedley, K (2010) *Psychological Therapy in Prisons and Other Secure Locations.* Devon: Willan.

A very useful source book that updates us on the core issues in prison psychotherapy written by real-life practitioners.

Pollock, M (1998) *Counselling Women in Prison.* London: Sage.

A bit dated but very informative, especially the chapters on treatment types and suggestions for future developments.

ONLINE RESOURCES

www.justice.gov.uk/inspectorate/hmi-prisons/ Prisons Inspectorate

www.justice.gov.uk/inspectorates/hmi-probation/ Probation Services Inspectorate

www.hmprisonservice.gov.uk HM Prison Service

www.howardleague.org The Howard League for Penal Reform

www.prisonreform.org

Counselling in Occupational Health (OH) and Employee Assistance Programmes (EAPs)

Frank Paice

CORE KNOWLEDGE

- Much of the UK workforce now has access to Occupational Health (OH) services, mostly through Employee Assistance Programmes (EAPs) bought in by employers.
- OH and EAP provision usually includes some form of counselling.
- OH and EAP clients provide a steadily growing source of work for independent counsellors, but accreditation/registration is an increasing requirement.
- Counsellors are usually self-employed and working in their own premises.
- Issues brought include both workplace-related and personal issues.
- Clients' perspectives (e.g. of bullying, stress, management style) can contrast with those of employers, with emphases on an early return to work after sickness absence and upon acceptance of the status quo.
- Most OH and EAP counselling is short term.
- Some career progression is available within EAPs.

INTRODUCTION

In this chapter, you will be introduced to the role played by counsellors in the provision of OH services and EAPs, in both private and public sectors. Those who employ counsellors in this sector almost always seek counsellors who have obtained accreditation and it is therefore unusual for newly qualified counsellors to be working in OH or for EAPs. Typically, one of the UK's largest EAP providers requires five years' post-qualification experience (**www.rightcorecare.co.uk**).

Nevertheless, it is hoped that the information provided here will be sufficient to inform those who already have the required experience, to encourage trainees to consider whether they might work in the future in this varied and rewarding sector, and also to draw to the attention of trainers and teachers some of the particular needs of trainees who may eventually enter this field of work. You will be shown some of the issues OH and EAP clients might bring to a counsellor. These can range from the specifically work-related to the personal. The chapter will present you with some of the situations you would be likely to face in OH or EAP work. Because OH and EAP work can be very short term, it will also challenge you to consider how you would work with clients whom you would see for as few as four sessions or less. More generally, it will invite you to consider how prepared you are for the demands of working as a self-employed therapist. The range of issues brought to the OH or EAP counsellor will be illustrated through examples of my work in East Anglia with clients referred by a range of employers, including those in the NHS, local government, and commercial and industrial concerns, both large and small. Most OH and EAP counsellors are self-employed and are contracted to see the clients who are referred to them on a sessional basis. This means that matters such as taxation, finding appropriate premises and the confidentiality of telephone and other communication are likely to be important considerations for counsellors working in OH and for EAPs. They will be looked at briefly towards the end of this chapter.

COUNSELLING IN OH AND FOR EAPs

As long ago as 1993, Michael Reddy wrote in *Counselling*, the then journal of the BACP, that *the centre of gravity of the counselling universe is moving inexorably to the workplace* (Reddy, 1993). OH counselling provision has continued to increase in recent years, although the major expansion has been in the presence of EAPs. The Employee Assistance Professionals Association (EAPA) claims that over 8.2 million employees in more than 5,000 UK organisations currently have access to the services of an EAP, including counselling (**www.eapa.org.uk**). As well as considerations of expediency, some employers also have an undoubted desire to express their concern for the welfare of the workforce by providing such services.

When EAPs are involved, some or all of the OH services provided by an employer are contracted out to a separate company, whose programme may offer such additional facilities as money advice and medical checks alongside counselling. Because of the economic downturn which began in 2008, some OH services are now being reduced in size and scope, with employers looking more and more to EAPs to provide a less costly service. In the case of counselling, this means a shift towards more use of telephone helplines and less direct face-to-face counselling.

The challenges presented in OH and EAP work are not unique, but some areas of concern are persistent. Recent media interest has drawn attention to the continued presence in the workplace of bullying and harassment. For example, in *The End of the Party,* recently serialised by *The Observer* (February 2010), Andrew Rawnsley alleged that Prime Minister Gordon Brown had persistently bullied his staff.

In at least one area of public service there is a steadily growing awareness of the cost to taxpayers of employees being off work with sickness and particularly with stress-related illness. Dr Steve Boorman's review into the health and well-being of NHS employees concluded that *NHS organisations must invest in the health and wellbeing of their workforce if they are to deliver sustainable, high-quality . . . patient care* (Boorman, 2009, p28). In the UK, there were 175 million working days lost to sickness absence in 2006, costing organisations around £650 per employee (**www.tuc.org.uk**).

Employers' desire to minimise the cost of absence is understandable, but counselling can be seen by some of them as little more than a means to this end. OH and EAP counselling is invariably time-limited and, in whatever orientation counsellors have been trained, there is sometimes pressure from employers to effect 'solutions', which may entail an early return to work. A counsellor's duty of care is ethically to her client, so she is bound to be aware of the potential conflict between the employer seeking an early return to work and the sometimes quite different needs and wishes of the client. While employers may view the culture of the workplace as enlightened, fair and efficient, clients can sometimes perceive the strategies employed by individual managers to encourage an early return to work as amounting to bullying and harassment.

Some employers are reluctant to use their own complaints and disciplinary procedures when grievances are raised over such matters, preferring to offer employees counselling to deal with their perceived 'stress' and then 'mediation' between the complainant and the colleague or manager against whom the grievance might otherwise have been brought. These differences of perspective are brought into even sharper focus by two inescapable facts. First, there is what the 'Guidelines for Ethical Practice' of the BACP call the counsellor's *fiduciary duty of trust* towards the client: the counsellor's first duty is towards that client. Second, though, it is the employer, through the provider of the OH service or EAP, who pays the counsellor.

REFLECTION POINT

Clients are sometimes suspicious of the counselling provided at the expense of the employer. They are concerned about confidentiality and possible 'reports back' to employers. By the same token, employers have been known to expect the counsellor to 'persuade' the client to go back to work, or to drop a grievance against a colleague. An awareness of the tension which can sometimes arise between the interests of the employer and the client is inescapable for the counsellor working in OH. EAPs can sometimes require counsellors to report behaviour which is disclosed through counselling, such as misuse of drugs and alcohol. There may be tensions for the counsellor, committed as she is to confidentiality and respect for the client's person, when such requests are offered as part of the contract between counsellor and provider – the so-called 'reporting concerns' requirement.

- How would being aware of these issues and tensions affect the way that you worked in an OH or EAP setting?
- How would you react to a requirement from a potential OH or EAP employer that – if offered the work – you would provide progress reports on clients, where details would be used to support or undermine their case in a grievance or disciplinary process?

ACTIVITY 7.1

Employers' Dignity at Work policies can sometimes be found on the internet. These policies often deal quite specifically with issues such as bullying, harassment, lack of appropriate communication and so on. Look up at least two such policies.

- What clues do these give you as to the types of concern which OH or EAP clients might bring to counselling regarding circumstances at work?

See if you can find on the internet the disciplinary and/or grievance policies of any major employers.

- What tensions and difficulties might you face as your client raises workplace issues related to any of these policies?

(Think about clients who are possibly struggling with relationships and the way they are managed, but who don't want to 'rock the boat'.)

THE DEVELOPMENT OF OCCUPATIONAL HEALTH AND EAP PROVISION IN THE UK

In their Preamble to the Constitution of the World Health Organization (WHO) (1946), the founders of the newly formed organisation agreed that health was a state of complete physical, mental and social well-being and not merely the absence of disease and infirmity (**www.who.int/governance/eb/constitution/en**).

In the 1970s, the Robens Committee, whose report preceded the Health and Safety at Work Act of 1974, may be seen by some as somewhat less visionary, stating, *We have interpreted 'occupational health' as being concerned with preventing ill health through control of the working environment* (Paragraph 347).

However, in a 1998 report of The Occupational Health Advisory Committee (OHAC), part of the Health and Safety Executive (HSE), OH was described as including the effect of health on work, bearing in mind that good occupational health practice should address the fitness of the task for the worker, not the fitness of the worker for the task alone (**www.hse.gov.uk/ aboutus/meetings/iacs/ohac**).

In January 2001, the BACP produced its first major study of OH provision, subsequently updated in 2008. Professor John McLeod wrote in the report that:

> *There has been a steady growth over the past 20 years in the number of organisations making use of in-house workplace counselling services, Employee Assistance Programmes (EAPs) and other methods of arranging psychological support for workers.*
>
> (2008, p4)

HM government, international bodies such as the WHO, employers, professional associations and trade unions increasingly acknowledged the importance of safeguarding psychological health. In a document entitled *Improving Quality and Productivity at Work: European Union Strategy 2008–2012* the European Union also committed itself to more research into a range of occupational concerns, including, *illnesses and infections associated with psychological stress* (**http://eur-lex.europa.eu/en/index.htm**).

Increasing numbers of employers responded to the new legal requirements that they attend to the health of their employees, but some tensions remained. A 2007 report of The Confederation of British Industry (CBI) criticised GPs over the cost to their members incurred when employees attended appointments, such as those with doctors and counsellors in work time. The report quoted independent research by Boots, claiming that some 3.5 million working days were lost each year because of time spent at GP surgeries alone. The riposte of GPs was swift: *If its (CBI) members think their staff are seeking medical appointments without any real cause, that seems to point to the need for a better occupational health service* (**www.tuc.org.uk**).

Matters have moved some way within the past 15 years. In a ten-year strategy document *Securing Health Together* (2000), the HSE targeted a 30 per cent reduction in the number of work days lost due to work-related ill health. The report made clear that increasing access in the workplace to OH support, including the availability of counselling, was fundamental to all of the improvements which it advocated. However, the global recession has caused both commercial businesses and public sector employers to re-examine the cost of such provision as OH and EAPs. There is already growing evidence that, in the short to medium term, the resultant scaling-down is both challenging the achievement of the goals of *Securing Health Together* and also leading to a substantial reduction in the employment by OH and EAPs of sessionally paid counsellors.

THE RANGE OF COUNSELLING PROVISION THROUGH OH AND EAPs

In the second decade of the twenty-first century, a range of counselling services is on offer to a growing proportion of the workforce, either through OH provision or through EAPs. In a large regional acute hospital, employees referred for counselling through the NHS Trust's own OH centre are offered, within days, access to a minimum of six sessions with an independent accredited therapist. The same centre provides OH services, including counselling, to a significant number of other local employers, including district councils, retailers, manufacturers and one of the emergency services.

OH provision
1. A local government officer whose employer utilises a local OH service might, typically, have developed anxiety and stress through a combination of pressures at work and at home. This may have led the GP at her local practice to sign her off work for a period of two weeks. On returning to work, she discusses with a line manager the difficulty she is having in 'staying on top of things'.
2. Her manager may now suggest that she access the OH counselling service and, upon the employee's agreement, make the necessary arrangements with OH.
3. The referral is now processed by an OH adviser, who contacts the worker by telephone, takes down contact details and establishes that she would like to see a female counsellor. Six sessions of counselling will be offered. OH administration now contacts one of its list of independent counsellors, who contacts the local government officer and arranges a first session.
4. Counselling commences at the therapist's premises.

Table 7.1: OH provision: an example of the process.

Until recently, a mental health care trust neighbouring the acute trust referred to above provided a minimum of four sessions of counselling through the same scheme, as did one of the primary care trusts. In both cases, economic constraints have recently led these organisations to seek less costly provision. EAPs offer a range of service levels, among which there are some which cost employers significantly less than a full OH provision. Counsellors may also be paid less than they are by an OH service.

A number of major employers in the same locality retain the services of EAPs, where employees may be referred through an initial telephone contact system for a fixed maximum number of sessions of counselling with an independent therapist, ranging down to a lesser number of telephone sessions, depending upon the 'package' purchased by the employer.

Smaller employers, such as medium-sized local authorities, sometimes buy in some services for employees from organisations offering OH or EAP services, but pay independent therapists under a separate arrangement for the counselling sessions which may be required from time to time. Owners of businesses employing workforces of as few as a dozen or less will sometimes contact a local therapist and express concern about an employee. The employer may have found the counsellor through the yellow pages, or via the BACP website; more typically, s/he will have received a recom-

---

EAP packages

The following is an example of the two packages which a leading EAP provider sells to employers. These are much like those on offer from other comparable EAPs.

Option 1
Full EAP package offering a 24-hour Advice and Counselling telephone service providing access to counselling, information and advice on issues including legal, financial, consumer and personal matters. Also included are six face-to-face counselling sessions per person covered, where necessary.

Option 2
EAP offering a 24-hour Advice and Counselling telephone service providing access to counselling, information and advice on issues including legal, financial, consumer and personal matters. Face-to-face counselling sessions can be purchased 'as and when your employees need them', or in bundles of 25 (any counselling sessions not used can be carried over to the subsequent contract term).

(**www.aviva.co.uk/healthcarezone/company**)

Table 7.2: Examples of EAP packages.

mendation from a friend or colleague. An arrangement is then made either for the employee to attend sessions, for which the invoice is sent to the business or, in some cases, sessions will be part paid for by the employer, with the remainder of the cost being borne by the client.

BECOMING AN OH OR EAP COUNSELLOR

Newly qualified counsellors seeking employment will need to search for information about jobs using a wide variety of means. The professional journals provide information about some employment opportunities, but they rarely include those in OH and with EAPs. *Therapy Today,* the current BACP journal, recently (2010: Vol. 21 (1)) carried 17 advertisements seeking qualified counsellors. None of these was for work with OH services or EAPs.

Finding work in an OH service or an EAP

Many counsellors find work by informal means. Sometimes, this involves working initially without payment, while accumulating the number of supervised counselling hours necessary for accreditation, eventually receiving an offer of some work when a paid position becomes vacant. On other occasions, a supervisor or colleague will pass on information about work which has become available.

REFLECTION POINT

With compulsory HPC registration looming, counsellors completing their training or degree courses are under increasing pressure to secure accreditation at the earliest opportunity and most OH or EAP providers will ask for a further two to three years' post-qualification experience.

- How is an awareness of the length of post-qualification experience required likely to affect any interest you might have in OH/EAP work?

ACTIVITY 7.2

Consider how you would view working unpaid after qualifying, in a service where other counsellors are paid and where clients may be paying full fee, in order to be able to apply eventually for this kind of work, as well as for accreditation. Look up some of the EAPs operating in your area and see what opportunities for employment there are at present.

Routes into OH or EAP work
1. Rachel completed more than150 hours of unpaid counselling practicum while undergoing training. Some of these hours were worked in a counselling service run by a charitable trust. As well as working elsewhere upon qualifying, Rachel continued at the service as a post-qualification intern (still unpaid) until she was eligible to apply for accreditation. She was told by the director of the service that an EAP was recruiting locally. She contacted the EAP and was eventually interviewed over the telephone. Within her first six months of working with this company, she saw five clients, for between two and six sessions each.
2. André had been accredited for two years when his supervisor, herself an independent therapist working for the local hospital-based OH service, told him that a further counsellor was required by the organisation. Specifically, the OH service was sometimes told by clients – male and female – that they preferred a male therapist. The only male counsellor attached to the organisation had recently left. After a quite rigorous interview with the service co-ordinator, André began to receive client referrals. Within a year, he was averaging eight counselling sessions per week with the service's clients.
3. Pat, a counsellor of seven years' experience, found the details of an EAP through its website and initially telephoned a member of its clinical team to ask for further details. She then applied on-line to become one of its counselling affiliates and was asked two weeks later to provide the details of two professional referees. Within a month, she was accepting clients and about a fifth of her work now comes via this provider.

Table 7.3: Examples of routes into OH or EAP work.

Probably the best place to find out more about working with EAPs is via providers' websites. A list of some major UK providers' websites is given at the end of the chapter, as are contact details for the EAPA, a source of further information about this sector of work.

Seeking EAP work via a provider's website
1. Upon logging on to the website of one EAP provider, the prospective affiliate is informed: 'We are always interested in hearing from skilled counsellors wishing to join our network of Chartered and Registered Psychologists and Counsellors'.
2. In this case, the potential EAP counsellor then provides basic personal details and responds to a series of questions about training, qualifications, length of experience (minimum five years' post-qualification), accreditation and location.
3. On completion and submission of the on-line form, she next awaits contact from the company and an indication of whether work is available.
4. The question of location is of importance: EAP providers seek to have sufficient coverage in a locality to enable them to find a suitable affiliate when making referrals, wherever a client may live. A relatively short journey for the client to the affiliate's premises is the ideal.

Table 7.4: The process of seeking EAP work via a provider's website.

Case study 7.1   Client referrals – occupational health

Jill is an experienced paramedic working with a regional ambulance service. In her early forties and a single parent, Jill derives tremendous satisfaction from her work. She has repeatedly faced appalling carnage and injury when attending road accidents on the stretch of motorway near the city where she lives. Her two daughters are in their late teens and still at school. Jill recently left a relationship with a man who flew into rages and hit her. She found it very difficult to leave the relationship, because of her fear of him, and of being alone.

In the past few weeks, Jill has begun to experience anxiety attacks, seemingly associated with work. On two recent call-outs to multiple-vehicle road accidents on the motorway, she has become increasingly fearful and agitated as her colleague has driven them to the scene of the accident. On the second occasion, she 'froze' at the scene and was unable to leave the ambulance. Eventually, she was given a lift back to the ambulance station in a police car. Her GP says she is both anxious and depressed and has prescribed medication. Her co-worker is very short-tempered and irritable with her and has said, in front of colleagues, that he believes she is unfit for work. Jill's widowed mother has advanced symptoms of dementia and there is pressure from her two brothers for her to move, with her daughters, into the capacious family home and care for their mother.

Jill's station manager is conscious of her situation and supportive, although largely unaware of what she went through with her partner. Following the latest episode on the motorway, he wants her to be assessed for her fitness to work by OH and makes the necessary appointment for her. She goes to the OH offices and sees a staff doctor, who interviews her and assesses her. She tells him about the anxiety attacks and also about both her relationship and her mother. He asks her to see her own GP again and have herself 'signed off' to give herself time to recover from what she has been dealing with. He also asks her to see one of the independent counsellors who see clients for OH.

Jill's details are passed, by an OH administrator, to Jeff, an experienced counsellor, who telephones Jill and arranges with her the first of six counselling sessions. Jill's counselling takes place at his premises in the city, which Jeff rents with three other therapists. The sessions last for 50 minutes each.

After the six sessions, and being signed off for almost two months, Jill is making progress with Jeff's help, but is not ready to return to work and Jeff requests three more sessions, which the OH administration clears with the ambulance trust.

Eleven weeks after the beginning of her sick leave, Jill – whose mother is now in a nursing home – begins a phased return to work, beginning with three days' 'light duties' at the ambulance station. After five further weeks, followed by a week's annual leave to coincide with the girls' half-term holiday, Jill returns to full duties, combined with a short period of in-service training.

Jill's assessment is that she had been demoralised by her mother's rapid decline and defeated by her situation with the former partner. Her situation had been compounded by a stressful and demanding job. She has experienced no anxiety attacks for more than two months and feels certain that counselling has been a big help.

Clients are often referred by OH providers without their being previously seen or assessed – either by an OH physician, or by a qualified nurse/adviser. Such clients' first contact with the counsellor to whom they are referred is effectively the first opportunity there has been for them to experience any form of assessment. This is often the point at which a counsellor's prior experience, and capacity to sit with a full-on 'unburdening' from the client is most called into use.

REFLECTION POINT

- OH work may present the counsellor with a client about whom she knows little, other than a phrase or two from the administrator, such as, 'It's a domestic issue and you are asked not to leave messages on her land-line,' or, 'It's a bullying issue at work, but I understand there has also been a bereavement.' This can leave the counsellor completely unprepared for the nature or intensity of what the client brings in her first session.

- OH work with health service employees frequently brings issues into the counselling room which are associated with the extremities of human experience, such as painful death, the loss of a very young infant, trauma and severe illness.

ACTIVITY 7.3

- Reflect upon how much use you currently make of prior knowledge about a client, gained from assessments done by others and from notes. What is your preference – to be well-briefed before meeting a client, or to be without prior information and entirely open to whatever the client brings?
- Make a list of factors in your previous life experience and training and practice so far that would enable you to sit with the extremities of a client's experience. Are you able to balance acceptance, empathy and honesty in such a way as to be 'enough' for a client in crisis?

Case study 7.2   Client referrals – Employee Assistance Programmes

Peter is 53 and works in the off-shore oil industry, where he supervises a team of 12 fitters in physically demanding all-weather work. He is generally away on the rig for three weeks, and then at home for two. In a second marriage, to a solicitor, he has a son from his first wife and another from an early relationship. His wife, 16 years his junior, has no children.

Last year, Peter developed early prostate cancer and was effectively treated using laser surgery. He currently has follow-up tests every three months. Peter has been the butt of some fairly insensitive humour on the rig, and is experiencing difficulties in intimacy with his wife Jennifer, who very much wants to be pregnant. Jennifer is the soul of empathy and gentle encouragement, but Peter's all-round confidence is at a very low ebb. He tells his general manager that he is considering leaving the drilling company. After much cajoling, the general manager finally manages to persuade Peter to telephone the EAP helpline to which he has in the past steered more than one employee under his supervision. The company buys in a very minimal package from the provider.

Peter speaks for almost 40 minutes to a duty telephone counsellor, who takes detailed notes, which he passes to the duty clinical case manager, Shelley, who is a very experienced senior accredited counsellor and supervisor. Shelley approves the case and passes the file to the referral team, who contact a counselling affiliate and inform her that Peter may have two sessions of face-to-face counselling, in keeping with Peter's firm's contract with the provider.

Colleen works out of a therapy centre in the small town near which Peter and Jennifer live. Peter is in his third week of sickness leave and his fifth off the rig. Colleen has a detailed set of notes in front of her when Peter arrives, taken down from her telephone conversation with the referral team member.

Peter breaks down completely once he and Colleen are in her consulting room. It seems to Colleen that the detail in her notes would be enough substance for a dozen sessions, but by the end of this first meeting, it has emerged that Peter's father died five years ago. He had been the 'rock' for his mother and his siblings, never showing any sign of breaking under the pressure they all laid on him. As he leaves, she reminds him that they have just one session left.

Some employers purchase packages from EAPs where a minimum of six face-to-face sessions of counselling are available, and are prepared to pay for several more where absolutely necessary. Other employees find themselves encouraged to unburden to a counsellor, only to discover that there are only one or two sessions left. It is not unknown for a major company to purchase just one face-to-face session.

REFLECTION POINT

Counselling training courses can be geared to the notion of the open-ended availability of as many sessions as are necessary for a client. Equally, they can include solution-focused and short-term approaches. It is almost unheard of for OH and EAP clients to be granted limitless counselling. Whatever their orientation, counsellors find themselves working with clients within the constraints imposed by the economic circumstances and the policies of the employer. Referral on, and an awareness of when it is necessary to make a referral, is sometimes an absolute duty within the relationship between client and counsellor. For example, a client whose issues are largely concerned with a deeply embedded eating disorder, or are psycho-sexual in nature may prove to have needs beyond the resourcefulness of even the most experienced and skilful generalist counsellor.

ACTIVITY 7.4

- Return to case study 7.2 relating to Peter. Reflect upon any ethical or other dilemmas thrown up by the combination of his complex presenting issues with

the limit of two sessions imposed by his employer. Look at the Ethical Guidelines of your accrediting body and consider what particular considerations need to be borne in mind should Colleen be asked by Peter to continue with him on a private basis.
- Consider the combination of matters with which Peter is dealing and how, in Colleen's position, you might see Peter moving forward. What referral opportunities are there in your area?

THE NUTS AND BOLTS OF SELF-EMPLOYMENT

You are likely to spend at least part of your time after qualification working in an internship, or some other voluntary position. If you are fortunate, you may also find salaried employment in which you can use your skills as a counsellor. OH and EAP counsellors are very frequently self-employed. It may be useful to look briefly at some issues that self-employed status inevitably raises.

Premises

A quick scan of small advertisements in publications like *Therapy Today* reveals advertisements for rooms, with rentals ranging from £50 per day in London to £5 per session in the rest of the UK. Generally speaking, rooms can be found in most localities for sessional rental. Experienced counsellors and supervisors, or people working for organisations like *Relate,* often know where there is a room to be let on that basis. They may also know of rooms which are available for a day or two each week. Rooms of this nature vary from those in houses which have been divided into four or five consulting rooms with shared (voluntary) reception facilities and a waiting room to serviced offices in larger buildings, with reception, telephone and appropriate waiting room thrown in for around £100 per month for one day a week. At less than £25 a day, or around £5 per session for a fully employed counsellor, such rooms can represent the best value. If you are taking EAP and OH clients, bear in mind that not everyone will be happy to be seen going into a 'holistic therapy centre', or a building showing advertisements for palm-readings.

Communications

Self-employed counsellors working for OH and EAPs need a secure and confidential telephone line. Sometimes, you will need to switch on a voice-mail or answerphone device, where your voice is reassuringly recognisable to the client. Such a device needs to be confidential, preferably with a 'sound off' switch and locked away in a cupboard or drawer. It is not appropriate to share a telephone with housemates or other family members, who may answer your client's calls. A separate mobile or dedicated land-line is strongly recommended! Similarly, email addresses available to clients should not be those shared with other people in our lives.

Finances

If you have not been self-employed before, do not fear the tax authorities! Even without the expensive services of an accountant, you can complete your annual tax return on-line and discover your tax bill quite easily in less than half an afternoon! In order to separate income from personal and household monies, it is strongly recommended that a separate bank account be opened, through which all income can be passed: most banks operate easy-to-use on-line accounts. HM Revenue and Customs (HMRC) have, for some time, run workshops on 'Becoming self-employed'. Details can be found on the HMRC website.

These workshops cover such concerns as registering your self-employment, National Insurance contributions for the self-employed, keeping business records for tax/NI purposes, completing the tax return and on-line services. BACP does offer leaflets on some aspects of working independently as a counsellor, but has no plans to replicate the information already provided by HMRC.

SO, IF I'M GOING THERE FROM HERE, WHERE WOULD I GO FROM THERE?

In the wake of the economic downturn, opportunities for work with public service-based OH providers may be fewer and further between during the second decade of the century. By contrast, work with EAPs looks set to increase. Once established in OH or EAP work, some counsellors may wish to consider the possibility of using their experience to take on more responsibility.

Progression in OH services

Some public OH services (predominantly run by hospital trusts) recruit accredited and experienced counsellors to take on the task of assessing the need of clients for counselling. However, the general tendency is for OH services to be run by career administrators and people with nurse adviser backgrounds. Nurse advisers will usually be nurses with at least a Registered General Nurse qualification, and not infrequently a nursing degree. They will usually also possess a post-registration qualification up to diploma or degree level. Counsellors will only usually be appointed to such posts where they also have some, if not all, of these qualifications.

Progression in EAPs

As well as self-employed counsellors whom they employ as affiliates, EAP providers also recruit experienced therapists in salaried positions to provide a help-line assessment response to clients, and also as referrers, communicating with affiliate counsellors. A more senior role is that of the clinical case manager, whose decisions are based on the initial information provided by clients, and who ultimately decides whether clients should be referred for face-to-face counselling, where employers have purchased this facility.

CHAPTER SUMMARY

The creation of counselling provision in the workplace through OH and EAPs arises largely through the concern of employers at absence and ineffectiveness caused by psychological ill-health. The limited provision of some form of psychological therapy has proved expedient both in reducing absence and in improving effectiveness. Providing counselling for employees can also be an expression of the employer's concern for the welfare of the workforce. Working as a counsellor in this setting is likely to require prior experience and accreditation. Among the constraints upon counsellors who work in this area is its short-term nature. Employers often expect counselling to encourage an early return to work. Some expect it to keep employees 'on-side'. Working as a counsellor in OH and EAPs can be both challenging and rewarding, and can provide a core of fairly consistent work while a private practice is being built up, as well as a real breadth of experience in terms of the range of clients and their issues. Despite economic constraints, it appears to be a growth area of work for qualified counsellors, offering them both income and some possibility of progression.

SUGGESTED FURTHER READING

Coles, A (2003) *Counselling in the Workplace.* Buckingham: Open University Press.

McLeod, J (2001; updated 2008) *Counselling in the Workplace.* Lutterworth: BACP.

A comprehensive survey of the research into workplace counselling.

Petersen, G, Pickvance, S, Kirby, P et al. (2007) *Occupational Health: Dealing with the issues.* London: Trades Union Congress.

ONLINE RESOURCES

http://eur-lex.europa.eu/en/index.htm European Union Law.

www.eapa.org.uk The Employee Assistance Professionals Association.

www.hse.gov.uk Health and Safety Executive.

www.nhshealthandwellbeing.org NHS Health and Wellbeing.

www.nhsplus.nhs.uk NHS Plus.

www.unionlearn.org.uk Trades Union Congress website for training, including OH.

www.who.int/en/ World Health Organization

Some EAP providers:

www.aviva.co.uk/healthcarezone/company Aviva.

www.axa-icas.com AXA ICAS.

www.employeeassistanceprogramme.com/bupa.htm BUPA.

www.ppcworldwide.com PPC Worldwide.

www.rightcorecare.co.uk Right Corecare.

Some OH providers:

www.hantsfire.gov.uk/theservice/occhealth.htm Hampshire Fire and Rescue service.

www.hmrc.gov.uk/bst/advice-team-events/work1.htm HMRC.

www.nlg.nhs.uk/services/occupational_health/default.asp North Lincolnshire and Goole NHS Foundation Trust.

www.nnuh.nhs.uk Norfolk and Norwich University Hospitals Foundation Trust.

www.westyorkshire.police.uk West Yorkshire Police force.

www.york.nhs.uk/ York Hospitals NHS Foundation Trust.

CHAPTER 8

Counselling within an IAPT context

Fredrick Asare and Paul O'Sullivan

CORE KNOWLEDGE

- Working in compliance with the National Institute for Health and Clinical Excellence (NICE) guidelines is an integral part of the Improving Access to Psychological Therapies (IAPT) ethos, particularly in terms of applying evidence-based psychological therapies.
- The professional infrastructure of IAPT allows for these psychological therapies to be delivered within a stepped-care model, as recommended by the NICE guidelines.
- The nature of IAPT means counsellors predominately work autonomously, often in a fairly mobile capacity seeing patients at more than one base on any given day.
- IAPT counsellors are usually expected to provide counselling within a Cognitive Behavioural Therapy (CBT) framework.
- One of the characteristics of IAPT is the emphasis on working in an outcome-focused and evidence-based manner. Outcome measures are used extensively to evaluate the success and effectiveness of counselling.

INTRODUCTION

Primary care services within the NHS have seen a significant expansion in the field of mental health since 2006. This nationwide development was preceded by a view that there was a shortage of counsellors providing evidence-based psychological therapy for mental health issues in the UK. The IAPT initiative has since been gradually rolled out whereby the government is attempting to improve access to psychological therapies through increased funding and more efficient services. IAPT is aimed at reducing mental health issues in the UK through an increased and more tailored provision of CBT. Such an impetus has meant that the training, expectations, organisational structure and role of counselling in primary care have undergone considerable change. This is a large-scale project, which is yet in its infancy and has been surrounded by much controversy.

This chapter aims to orientate the reader towards explaining the rationale and inception of IAPT, as well as exploring the role of counsellors within the current primary care landscape. The chapter will start by outlining the history of IAPT, from its origins through to its implementation to date. This will be followed by a description of the training and qualification processes required in becoming an IAPT counsellor. In addition, issues linked to the everyday practicalities of counselling and training in this context will be considered. The reader will note that throughout the chapter a number of reflective learning points and examples from IAPT settings are provided. These are aimed at exploring the overall picture and challenges of coun- selling in IAPT but have been gathered mainly from the authors' clinical experience of counselling at the IAPT site within South Essex Partnership NHS Foundation Trust (SEPT).

HISTORY OF IAPT

The IAPT initiative evolved from suggestions made in the Labour Govern- ment's 2005 General Election Manifesto (2005, p64), which proposed to increase investment and improve mental health services in the UK. The following year, Economist Lord Richard Layard (The Centre for Economic Performance at the London School of Economics, 2006) published an influential report that assessed the existing provision of psychological therapies in the treatment of depression and anxiety at primary care level. Layard found that only one in four people suffering from depression or chronic anxiety were receiving any form of treatment, and this would leave a sizeable percentage of the population at risk of experiencing enduring mental ill-health. Furthermore, Layard pointed out the significant financial cost that mental health issues have on the UK economy. The report also noted the NICE guidelines' assertion that evidence-based psychological therapies, such as CBT, should be available and applied in the treatment of depression and anxiety. Despite this, the NICE guidelines were sparingly implemented in primary care due to a lack of psychological therapists employed in this sector.

Layard concluded that in order to rectify this shortfall, several changes would need to be implemented. First, the report recommended the establishment of a centrally led and centrally funded framework for a set initial period until the service was fully operational, at which time the IAPT service would be decentralised and managed locally. It was predicted that 10,000 new psychological therapists would be required to meet the increased demand, along with a specifically tailored postgraduate training scheme to establish a skilled workforce.

The proposed solution to the lack of provision put forward by Layard was widely supported and resulted in funding being granted to set up two national IAPT demonstration sites to trial a new Primary Care Trust (PCT) psychological therapies service. Doncaster PCT and Newham PCT were selected as demonstration sites and went live in 2006. The remit of both Doncaster and Newham PCTs was to test the effectiveness of providing evidence-based psychological therapy services to those in the community who needed them. An additional rationale behind this initiative was to support and maintain people with mental health issues in employment. Alternatively, for those members of the community currently unemployed and suffering distress, the IAPT initiative would seek to help them to gain employment.

Primary aims

The primary aims of IAPT are:

- to improve access to psychological therapies for clients suffering from psychological distress;
- to reduce the number of people in the UK suffering from common mental health issues, e.g. depression and anxiety disorders;
- to reduce the social effects and financial costs of mental health issues;
- to reduce unemployment rates.

Following the demonstration sites' first year of service, Layard and his colleagues evaluated their performance (Clarke et al., 2008). Both sites were deemed to have made substantial achievements, with both showing an impressive number of people accessing the service and receiving treatment. This further supported the effectiveness of using CBT in delivering short-term therapy. Effects on employment were also encouraging, with a number of the treated population returning to employment within the year. One of the most significant findings in the evaluation by Layard was that one in five people seen in Newham entered the service by means of the trialled self-referral process. This was a route into the service that was not previously available. Notably, those who self-referred tended to present with more enduring problems and closely matched the ethnic mix of the local population. These findings demonstrated the potential of IAPT in reaching sections of the population who were not adequately catered for under the pre-existing NHS arrangements for mental health.

Mindful of the personal, societal and economic costs of mental illness, one of the aims of the IAPT programme was to offer psychological interventions that were accessible to the whole community. Supplementing the early successes of the demonstration sites, the IAPT programme was extended in 2007/08 to include 11 Pathfinder sites that aimed to further develop ways to improve access to IAPT services. Around the same period, Special Interest Groups (SIGs) were also established to support the designated IAPT Pathfinder sites in exploring the needs of particular groups within its local population (Department of Health, 2008a). The SIGs were formed with the intention of addressing any specific barriers to access and therefore making psychological interventions more readily available to all those who may benefit from them.

The outcome of the Pathfinder sites, and specifically the SIGs, highlighted several inter-community barriers that required addressing to ensure the IAPT programme remained accessible for people in the community – one common recommendation cited the need for proper and effective engagement. A suggested method of achieving this was to ensure that successful and unsuccessful pathways were identified early in treatment so that effective engagement in therapy could be facilitated and maintained. A further proposal suggested that IAPT services take a flexible approach when providing treatment, with the patient's needs central to this flexibility. For example, the parent of a newborn child might require home visits or for appointments to be scheduled to coincide with the baby's routine or their carer's availability. The proposals also highlighted the need to establish collaborative working relationships with local community organisations and other health professionals to assist in the patient's engagement and overall treatment.

REFLECTION POINT

Consider the area where you live.

- What minority groups live in your area?
- What more could be done in reaching out to these groups to make psychological therapies more accessible?
- Do you think there is a need for a free-for-all NHS service to be flexible in meeting the diverse needs of a community or should the responsibility lie with the individual to fit into the provided service?

Now consider your own position as a professional or a potential client accessing IAPT.

- Remembering what IAPT stands for, Improving Access to Psychological Therapies, what more do you think could be done to make psychological therapies more accessible?
- How might you work to make therapy services more flexible and encourage greater engagement?

THE NATIONAL ROLLOUT OF THE IAPT PROGRAMME

Following the early successes, the IAPT service was rolled out nationally in 2008. PCTs from the country's ten strategic health authorities were selected to establish the IAPT programme in its first full year, with a gradual expansion of the service during the subsequent years. In order to facilitate the nationwide expansion, an increase of approximately 700 therapy workers were employed in the first two years of service, with an estimated 3,600 therapists being delivered by the IAPT training programmes by 2010/11.

With the government's commitment to the IAPT programme, additional funding was allocated to increase services over the initial three years of the implementation process. The structure of the funding was phased in order to account for the increased costs as the therapeutic workforce was gradually trained. The government allocated £33 million to be made available to support the initial phase of the IAPT implementation process in 2008/09. Thereafter, a further £70 million to a total of £173 million was allocated to fund and maintain the IAPT programme each year between 2009 and 2011 (Department of Health, 2008b). These funds were used to deliver the extensive IAPT training programmes required to provide the necessary number of suitably qualified psychological therapists for the progressive expansion of the IAPT services.

THE STEPPED-CARE MODEL

The National Institute for Health and Clinical Excellence (NICE) is an organisation that is concerned with regulating the standards to which healthcare is delivered in the UK. One of the key arguments in Lord Layard's report was the lack of application of the NICE guidelines, which aim to provide people with mental illness the choice of psychological therapy, thus alleviating the national economic and social effects of depression and anxiety disorders. With due consideration given to Lord Layard's observations, the principal aim of the IAPT programme is to support PCTs in implementing NICE guidelines. The professional structure of counselling in IAPT services is adapted to fit with the stepped-care model, as recommended by the NICE guidelines. The stepped-care model has two fundamental principles (CSIP Choice and Access Team, 2008).

- Appropriate treatment should always have the best chance of delivering positive outcomes, while ensuring the burden placed on patients is kept at a minimum.
- Systematic review to detect and act on non-improvement to enable stepping up to more intensive treatments, stepping down where a less intensive treatment becomes appropriate, and stepping out when alternative or no treatment is deemed appropriate.

The stepped-care model proposes an approach to mental health care within the NHS whereby clients are treated depending on the severity of their symptoms, ranging from steps 1 to 5. This model sets out to deliver the lowest appropriate intervention with a 'stepping up' of the level of care when needed. The idea behind this is to optimise resources as well as provide counselling, which is suitable and tailored to individual clients' needs (**www.iapt.nhs.uk/services**).

Step 1, the entry level into the IAPT service, includes the initial assessment of the individual's presenting problem and, if necessary, a period of watchful waiting. Steps 2 and 3 offer psychological interventions on both an individual and group basis. The low-intensity therapy services at step 2 level comprise computerised Cognitive Behavioural Therapy (cCBT), guided self-help, behavioural activation and psycho education. The severity of disorders treated in step 2 range from mild to moderate and include depression, panic disorder, Generalised Anxiety Disorder (GAD) and Obsessive-Compulsive Disorder (OCD). Step 3 incorporates the high-intensity interventions, which predominantly applies a CBT approach to the treatment of mild to moderate depression, social phobia, Post-Traumatic Stress Disorder (PTSD), as well as the disorders covered in step 2. Alongside the therapeutic services, people seeking support also have access to additional services, including employment advisers, a GP adviser and links to other services such as housing, benefits and drugs advice.

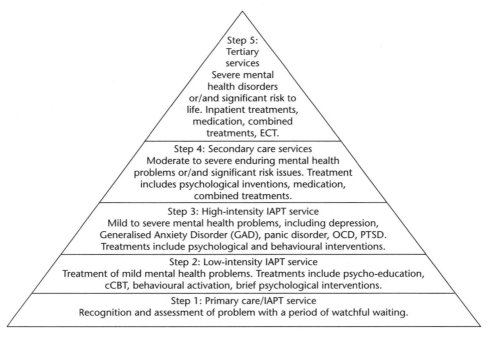

Figure 8.1: The stepped-care model of delivery.

ACTIVITY 8.1

Read the following client descriptions and consider what would be the most appropriate step to refer them to on the stepped-care model.

a. Julie-Ann self-referred to the service having seen an IAPT poster in her GP surgery. She is a 48-year-old married woman who works as a solicitor for a small, yet very busy property legal firm. Following a recent promotion at work that requires her to work long hours and lead many team and client meetings, she has begun to feel increasingly stressed and anxious, especially when chairing meetings. She says that since her promotion she has found it difficult to sleep and often wakes up in the morning 'stressing about work'. She says that although she is able to continue working she is concerned that her work might suffer if she doesn't get help soon.

b. Matthew is a 30-year-old man who was referred to IAPT by his GP having reported feeling low and generally hopeless since being made redundant 12 months ago. Matthew is currently prescribed a course of anti-depressants and has been taking the medication for the past three months. He reports having little pleasure in doing things and spends the majority of his time at home due to 'having no cash to go out with mates' and feeling self-conscious about his physical appearance. Matthew also claimed to have had thoughts of taking his own life when he was first made redundant, but has not experienced similar thoughts since taking the anti-depressants.

c. Terry is a 72-year-old retired man who was signposted to the service by his GP. Terry has complained of feeling low in mood and highly anxious since he was involved in a serious road accident ten months ago. He claims that following the accident he has had trouble sleeping, waking up suddenly most nights often after having a disturbing dream about the accident. Terry states that he has rarely driven since the accident, often preferring to walk or cycle, and when he does drive he says he feels 'very nervous and edgy the whole time'.

COMMENT

a. Considering Julie-Ann's presentation she seems most suitable for low-intensity treatment in step 2. It is her first episode of anxiety and the onset is relatively recent. She has no previous history of mental health issues and seems able to manage her stress proficiently.

b. Because of the severity of Matthew's depression, and considering the seemingly enduring nature of his condition, he is probably most suitable for high-intensity treatment at step 3. He also presents with some risk issues that would require more intensive interventions and monitoring than would be offered in step 2.

c. The nature of Terry's current difficulties would seem to suggest that he is experiencing symptoms of PTSD. This is a highly debilitating condition that would be appropriate for step 3 high-intensity interventions. Interventions for this condition would require longer and more intensive counselling, such as cognitive restructuring and exposure work.

PROFESSIONAL STRUCTURE

One of the fundamental principles underpinning the selection of suitable counsellors to IAPT services is the recruitment of a workforce that reflects the diverse cultural and socioeconomic background of the local community (Clark et al., 2008). Although there are those counsellors in IAPT settings who may deliver alternative therapies, the vast majority currently provide CBT. Counsellors working in IAPT are therefore undergoing, or have completed training in CBT and are, broadly speaking, divided into the following four categories.

1. Psychological Wellbeing Practitioner (PWP) (formerly referred to as Low Intensity Worker).
2. Psychological Wellbeing Practitioner Trainee.
3. High Intensity Worker.
4. High Intensity Trainee.

PSYCHOLOGICAL WELLBEING PRACTITIONERS (PWPs)

Psychological Wellbeing Practitioners and the associated trainee posts are primarily concerned with treating clients in step 2 suffering from mild symptoms of depression or anxiety. The interventions delivered by PWP counsellors tend to be less intensive and typically last for four to six sessions. The focus at this stage is on self-management rather than intensive psychological interventions. While PWPs see clients face to face, the needs of some clients may be appropriately treated through online or telephone contact (Ghosh, 2009). However, due to the nature of the work that these counsellors carry out, they tend to hold larger caseloads than High Intensity Workers, with some PWPs carrying up to 45 cases simultaneously. The types of interventions delivered by PWPs include psycho-education, guided self-help, bibliotherapy, and cCBT. In addition, they provide clients with support and information with regards to unemployment issues and pharmacological treatments such as the range of different anti-depressants and their expected effectiveness. However, this is purely in an advisory capacity, with the final decision and consultation resting with the GP or psychiatrist prescribing such medication. Moreover, PWPs are expected to assess clients for risk and refer on when presented with issues outside the scope of their professional competencies.

The training to become a fully fledged PWP takes one year of studies at university alongside clinical work with clients. Typically, trainee PWPs attend taught modules at university one day per week with the remaining days of their working week spent doing casework. During training, the size of caseloads is smaller than is expected upon qualification. Trainees will also be more closely supervised during this time. The taught components of PWP training are aimed at developing skills and competency in assessing and treating mild and common mental health issues. Trainee PWPs undertake modules, coursework and practical assessments focused on building and maintaining therapeutic relationships, assessment skills, as well as the delivery of evidence-based low-intensity interventions within a healthcare context. The training to become a PWP leads to a postgraduate certificate. At present, the institutes delivering this training are not regulated or accredited by relevant professional bodies, as is the case with the High Intensity training. This issue is currently under discussion within the Oversight Group Accreditation for IAPT training (OGAIT).

The trainee PWP post is intended for graduates with relevant work experience in mental health. However, some applicants are accepted without an undergraduate degree when they are able to demonstrate adequate experience and skills in mental health work. While an interest and relevant experience are required, trainee PWPs are recruited from a wide range of professional backgrounds. The prerequisites to working as a PWP are:

- an ability and willingness to form professional relationships with a large number of people;
- being able to manage a large caseload;
- the ability to grasp and deliver low-intensity counselling predominately based on the principles of CBT;
- an aptitude to work towards targets and work in a systematic and efficient manner.

After working as a qualified PWP for two years (or less, if the necessary skills and competence have been acquired), counsellors are normally eligible to apply for a position as a trainee High Intensity Worker (HIW).

ACTIVITY 8.2

Many of the low-intensity interventions delivered by PWPs are internet-based and available online. Do an online search and list some of the most common internet-based interventions and in what instance they might be most beneficial.

REFLECTION POINT

The work that you are expected to undertake as a PWP is usually short term and highly goal-oriented. With this in mind, consider the following.

- How do you think working in IAPT will affect your ability to form therapeutic relationships with clients when working in a time-limited way?
- In what way would working collaboratively to achieve goals be important and how might this concept be applied in practice?

HIGH INTENSITY WORKERS (HIWs)

HI counsellors within IAPT deliver CBT to clients suffering from symptoms of depression and anxiety disorders, such as social anxiety, OCD and PTSD. The clients seen by HIWs are those suffering from moderate to severe mental health issues. The HI interventions are provided within a CBT framework in one-to-one or group settings. IAPT facilitates a range of therapeutic groups including those for depression, anxiety and eating disorders. The counselling provided by HI workers is time-limited and typically within the range of 8–12 sessions. HI workers are trained in assessing common mental health issues and associated risk issues in relation to clients' suitability for counselling. They are also expected to work in a collaborative manner with their patients, as well as demonstrate the ability to devise case formulations and treatment plans. The purpose of case formulations and treatment plans is to obtain an overall psychological profile of clients' distress and a plan of how such problems can be treated in an efficient and evidence-based manner. HI counsellors also provide supervision for HI trainees and, sometimes, PWPs. As a result of the focus on delivering high-intensity CBT interventions, these counsellors have smaller caseloads and see clients for longer than is expected for low-intensity interventions.

HI counselling aims to encourage clients to identify and challenge unhelpful thoughts and behaviours. These interventions are offered to clients suffering from symptoms deemed inappropriate for low-intensity therapy due to the severity of presenting problems. Alternatively, HI counselling can be offered when low-intensity interventions have already been tried without satisfactory results.

The training to become a High Intensity counsellor is a one-year full-time postgraduate course. HI trainees undertake taught modules at university two days per week as well as working clinically with clients the remaining days of the week. Upon completion, trainees are awarded an MSc in Cognitive Behavioural Therapy and are eligible to apply for accreditation with the British Association for Behavioural and Cognitive Psychotherapies (BABCP) as CBT therapists. During this training, tutor-led supervision and taught modules are aimed at developing competency and skills in delivering a variety of CBT interventions for specific mental health issues, as well as assessing clients in terms of risk and suitability for counselling. Trainees are also taught to work in an autonomous, evidence-based and outcome-focused fashion. In this regard, the training involves case reports, role play exercises, theoretical essays and assessment of audio recordings from therapy sessions.

Trainee HI workers are typically experienced in delivering counselling or other related therapeutic interventions. The training is aimed at post-graduates such as psychotherapists and counselling/clinical psychologists. There are also those with mental health experience from related fields, including nurses, occupational therapists, social workers and primary care therapists, who can demonstrate equivalence in academic and professional competence.

The professional structure outlined above accurately represents the organisational landscape in IAPT although local variations do exists. However, it is worth noting that the HI workers and PWPs often work alongside clinical/counselling psychologists as well as primary care therapists. Such clinicians tend to provide alternative or more generic forms of counselling such as psychodynamic, person-centred and integrative counselling.

The high and low modalities of counselling within IAPT

- HI counsellors provide more intensive and comprehensive CBT to clients with moderate distress on a one-to-one basis or in groups as well as providing supervision to colleagues.
- PWPs deliver low-intensity CBT interventions to a large number of clients typically suffering from mild symptoms of depression or anxiety for short periods of time.

Case study 8.1   Daniel

Daniel is a 23-year-old unemployed male who has self-referred for counselling after being prompted by his friends and family. He has scored relatively highly on outcome measures, particularly with regard to his anxiety levels. Considering Daniel's presenting problem and high outcome scores, he was referred to step 3 for high-intensity individual counselling. In his initial meeting with his counsellor, Daniel seems extremely shy and often avoids eye contact. He does, however, describe having suffered from social anxiety and panic attacks for most of his life but mentions that these symptoms have worsened since his relationship with his girlfriend ended 11 months ago. He reports periods when he avoids leaving his home due to anxiety of being laughed at or being embarrassed by making a fool of himself.

Daniel also claims that he often experiences panic attacks 2–3 times a day. The self-assessment that Daniel completed did not indicate any immediate risk concerns. However, while conducting a risk assessment at the first appointment, it transpires that he frequently feels suicidal and 'sometimes' cuts his arms to release his emotional distress.

During the continuous monitoring of risk issues in counselling, Daniel does not express any plan or intentions to end his life, although he does report that at times he feels it would be easier to just 'give up'. It transpires during counselling that Daniel grew up with a father who was violent and emotionally withdrawn. He also described being criticised when he was younger for not being as academically able as his older brother.

By collaboratively exploring Daniel's behavioural and thinking patterns, the counsellor managed to identify how he often seems to jump to conclusions or predict the outcome of unknown situations. He also appears to avoid situations with unknown people or asks his mum to answer his mobile phone for him. Although Daniel is initially resistant to challenging his thoughts and behaviours, he does eventually start to question some of these and is able to try out some new things by gradually exposing himself to fearful situations. Halfway through therapy, Daniel's GP speaks to the counsellor and reveals that he has noticed an abundance of recent cut marks on Daniel's forearms and expresses a concern for his well-being. The GP has mentioned to Daniel that he felt it was important that this was addressed in counselling and that he may need to break confidentiality and speak to his counsellor, to which Daniel agreed. He initially seems distressed by this conversation and is worried about being judged by others.

However, by being taught alternative strategies to deal with his anxiety, he is eventually able to reduce the frequency of self-harming as his overall anxiety levels gradually decrease during and after counselling. On ending counselling, Daniel describes feeling more able to cope with his anxiety and less inclined to self-harm through applying the techniques he has been taught. He does agree, however, to attend a psycho-education group for self-esteem in order to improve his negative beliefs about himself as well as continue to expose himself to social situations.

COMMENT

In this case, being able to gain Daniel's trust to identify and monitor his level of risk was crucial. Given his initial anxiety and presentation this was a challenging task. For many people, entering counselling may represent the first time they have disclosed what is going on for them. It may also be very difficult to talk about any suicidal thoughts with a relative stranger. Although Daniel's risk issues were contained through counselling, the communication between his GP and counsellor and subsequently Daniel, required careful negotiation but eventually became a turning point in the process. In the autonomous IAPT environment, the ability to liaise with other professionals is vital. In this case, the counsellor also kept clear notes with regard to the risk issues discussed and consulted his supervisor about this. Furthermore, issues around confidentiality and duty of care were discussed in detail with Daniel during the first appointment and were reiterated several times. Had there been any set-backs, these safety measures would have been crucial to demonstrate that the counsellor had practised in a safe and ethical manner.

REFLECTION POINT

- Considering Daniel's presenting problems, especially his suicidal thoughts and episodes of self-harm, how do you think you would manage his difficulties if you were his counsellor?
- Can you think of further ways to work with a client who presents with social anxiety?

PRACTICAL ISSUES

For the newly qualified counsellor, entering an organisation such as the NHS can feel similar to how Alice [in Wonderland] may have experienced her first moments when entering the rabbit-hole. The NHS is an enormous organisation; it is the second largest employer in Europe. It also has a particular culture, which is focused towards a medical approach to care (Smallwood, 2002). This means that counsellors need to understand some of the medical terminology and procedures related to counselling, as well as become familiar with an array of different services and referral procedures. It is, for example, important to know when and how to refer clients from primary to secondary care or where clients suffering from drug and alcohol problems can be signposted. Furthermore, counselling and psychotherapy have been influenced by humanistic values where each client is seen as unique and the expert on their own experience. This stands in contrast to the NHS, where clients often are referred to as patients with 'illnesses' that can be categorised into different disorders where the ultimate goal is to 'cure' (Lenihan and Iliffe, 2000). The field of counselling and the NHS as organisational structures, therefore, differ markedly in terms of the underpinning values and ideologies. This gap is one that requires some negotiation and adaptation on the part of the individual counsellor.

WORKING IN AN OUTCOME-FOCUSED SETTING WITH AN EMPHASIS ON CBT

CBT is a widely used and accepted model of counselling. It enjoys a prominent status within the mental health arena due to the empirical support that it has accumulated (Beck, 1991; Kuyken et al., 2009). One of the fundamental underpinnings of CBT is the assumption that psychological distress arises from the way people interpret events in their lives rather than the events themselves. CBT, therefore, strives to identify and challenge unhelpful thoughts and behaviours in a structured and systematic fashion. The success of CBT interventions is invariably evaluated according to a reduction in the symptoms of distress (Trower et al., 2007). It has, in this regard, become increasingly common to use a variety of outcome measures to evaluate the efficiency of CBT. These measures typically ask clients to rate their mood and psychological well-being in different domains.

The NICE guidelines recommend CBT as the first line of treatment for most mental health issues currently treated within IAPT. Counsellors are, therefore, expected to provide counselling within a CBT framework. There are plans at a later stage to expand IAPT services to include those counsellors who work in models other than CBT (Ghosh, 2009). The implication of this at present is that counsellors in IAPT are working within a framework in which they have trained and that is supported by a relatively large body of research. The potential caveat is that some counsellors may not agree with working within a single model of counselling such as CBT. They might instead find it beneficial to use techniques and ideas from a variety of frameworks.

This dilemma has been addressed by counsellors and psychotherapists in the past. Nuttall (2008) argues that working integratively provides a more sound and efficient platform for counselling. Opponents of such ideas tend to argue that different models of counselling are philosophically and ideologically incompatible (Norcross and Goldfried, 2005). This argument has also been extended to suggest that counsellors working integratively may run into problems when trying to conceptualise their understanding of clients and their problems (Hollanders, 1999). Regardless of one's views in this controversy, the current emphasis on working within a singular model of counselling is an issue for counsellors to consider before pursuing a career in IAPT. Furthermore, some of the clients who are referred to IAPT services do not always fit neatly into the categories of problems that are most suitably treated by CBT.

In general, it would seem that counselling has become increasingly influenced by resources and funding. Perhaps underpinned by the political and economic agenda, this trend is particularly evident in IAPT where there is a strong focus on working in a time-limited, efficient and outcome-focused manner. Most counsellors would probably agree that there is a shortage of supply and excess in demand. However, one of the principal aims of the IAPT service is to increase the potential for clients to access the service, such as offering extended evening and weekend opening hours (Department of Health, 2007). Such demands are evident in terms of the various outcome measures that are used and also in the ways that clients are assessed, the number of therapy sessions offered, and the distribution between high- and low-intensity counselling. One of the advantages of this system is that clients are subject to shorter waiting lists and counsellors are prompted to work in a more structured, efficient and goal-oriented manner.

These additional demands require IAPT counsellors to be highly skilled not only in their therapeutic work but also in case and time management. Another challenge for counsellors is to negotiate between organisational demands and clients' needs. Counsellors may find it a challenge to remain focused on developing quality therapeutic relationships within a highly target driven and goal-oriented setting.

OUTCOME MEASURES

One of the characteristics of IAPT is the emphasis on working in an outcome-focused and evidence-based manner. Outcome measures are used extensively to evaluate the success and effectiveness of counselling. A number of different assessment forms are used that ask clients to rate their psychological well-being (typically on a scale of 0–3) in different domains such as low mood and anxiety. The outcome measures use standardised scores that can be calculated relatively easily to give an overall indication of clients' psychological profile. While local variations exist, the three most frequently used outcome measures in IAPT settings are as follows.

1. Patient Health Questionnaire (PHQ9)
    The PHQ9 includes a number of questions about low mood and depression using questions such as *over the last 2 weeks how often have you been bothered by little interest or pleasure in doing things?* (Kroenke et al., 2001).
2. General Anxiety Disorder assessment (GAD7)
    The GAD7 relates to symptoms of anxiety by asking questions such as *how often over the last 2 weeks have you felt nervous, anxious or on the edge?* (Löwe et al., 2008).

3. Clinical Outcomes in Routine Evaluation (CORE)
   The CORE is a more global outcome measure concerned with overall psychological functioning as well as risk issues and is exemplified by questions such as *have you ever had thoughts of taking your own life or planned to do so? (Armstrong, 2010)*.

Outcome measures are normally completed prior to, during and after counselling. One of the advantages is that at assessment, they can help determine whether clients are appropriate for high- or low-intensity counselling and help the counsellor become aware of particular problem areas. Another useful advantage is that outcome measures can provide a sense of the client's progress or otherwise during the course of therapy. Clients may also find it rewarding to track their progress numerically. However, trying to quantify and rate psychological well-being can be problematic and does not always give an accurate understanding of client experiences. Furthermore, while relatively simple to use, the use of outcome measures places additional administrative demands on counsellors who are already managing large caseloads. In some instances, outcome measures can be difficult to use with clients who have limited ability to read or write.

REFLECTION POINT

CBT attempts to identify and challenge unhelpful ways of thinking and behaving with regard to specific problems such as depression. Therapeutic gain is assessed by means of outcome measures to see if psychological distress has reduced after counselling. Consider the following questions with regard to CBT and your own personal values.

- Is it possible to evaluate psychological well-being by means of numerical values obtained from outcome measures?
- How might your personal and therapeutic stance need to be adapted to fit into an IAPT setting, which can be highly target- and result-oriented?

ASSESSMENT AND RISK

Counselling services outside IAPT typically assess new clients in person. This enables the counsellor to make an informed decision about whether or not a client is suitable for the service offered. The counsellor can make an in-depth evaluation of the client's account as well as forming an impression of the client based on how they come across. However, as a result of trying to optimise efficiency, many IAPT sites have devised new ways of assessing and assigning clients to counsellors. These methods include online and telephone assessments, as well as pen and paper self-reports that can be sent via post. While these efforts have the potential to improve efficiency and cut down on administrative workloads, they also have some practical implications for counsellors. That is, counsellors will often be the first point of entry for new referrals and it is, therefore, important that continuous assessment is carried out to evaluate whether clients are appropriate for counselling in an IAPT setting. This is particularly true given that clients are assigned to high- or low-intensity counselling based on their scores on outcome measures as well as self-reported risk issues.

A further consideration for counsellors relates to risk and the potential for clients to be a danger to themselves or others. A considerable number of clients report having contemplated suicide at some point, with some disclosing that they have made previous attempts to end their life or have plans to do so. In some cases, clients may be referred to alternative services, such as secondary care, while also undergoing continuous and thorough risk assessments. Such procedures can be challenging within an IAPT setting due to the sheer volume of clients, the nature of assessments, and the mobile nature of the work with counsellors working from multiple sites. These issues further stress the importance for IAPT counsellors to work in a proactive and autonomous way, as well as having a thorough understanding of the various partner services and pathways within the NHS.

ACTIVITY 8.3

With such busy, and sometimes heavy, caseloads, counsellors need to engage in effective self-care and stress management to avoid burn-out and exhaustion. Consider your own self-care and stress management strategies.

- Which ones are particularly useful to you for dealing with distressing client issues?
- Which areas of your own well-being do you need to address to work effectively?

MANAGING TRAINING AND CLINICAL WORK

One of the challenges facing PWP trainees and High Intensity Trainees (HITs) is the intensity of working clinically alongside the requirements of writing essays, case studies and other academic tasks. Some IAPT services allocate extra time to trainees to manage academic demands in addition to the days they attend university. In the current financial climate, however, this is far from the norm. Trainees are faced with the additional pressure of evenings and weekends being taken up with completing coursework after a busy week of learning to implement CBT interventions in practice. Furthermore, many of the issues related to counselling within an IAPT context are covered at university in a formulaic and structured manner and the trainee counsellor is likely to encounter clinical issues that may not yet have been covered by their IAPT training. This means that counsellors will often have to cope with the stress of improvising in unknown territory. It could, for example, be challenging to work with symptoms of OCD before having engaged academically with the relevant theories and treatment protocols. Such issues require an adequate use of supervision, working autonomously, as well as being creative and resourceful. This is particularly true considering that qualified and trainee counsellors in IAPT settings often work independently and in isolation from fellow counsellors.

THE CHALLENGE OF WORKING AS A 'CONTRACT' COUNSELLOR

Working as a counsellor within an IAPT environment is in many respects a unique and challenging experience. The impetus inherent in IAPT has meant that counsellors are distributed to work from a number of busy sites such as GP surgeries, health centres, local community centres and resource centres. For someone who is not used to such environments it can initially feel hectic and stressful as well as different from the 'stereotypical' notion of counselling conducted in the calm, quiet confines of a private office. Counsellors often become a sort of 'contract counsellor', seeing a number of clients at one site and then more clients elsewhere, later in the day. Moreover, due to the large number of counsellors employed within IAPT and the expansion from previous services, there is limited office space in which to accommodate all counsellors. This factor, in conjunction with the mobile nature of counselling in this context, can result in counsellors experiencing a sense of working in isolation. For people accustomed to working in a team at a single location, it can take some time to get used to these arrangements.

The challenges of this environment require counsellors to form sound relationships with GPs, business managers, nurses, supervisors and other counsellors despite limited time for contact. Liaising and signposting to other services and professionals can be challenging, especially when communication is usually conducted via email or by phone. As many of the IAPT sites are relatively new, referral pathways and procedures have taken time to be established and have been somewhat difficult to implement. These challenges, however, present a varied and dynamic work environment that some counsellors find very stimulating and rewarding.

REFLECTION POINT

What do you think might be the implications of working in this environment in terms of your own professional development?

CONFIDENTIALITY

The ability to build rapport and a healthy therapeutic relationship is to a large extent underpinned by the client's ability to trust their counsellor whereby information that is shared is handled with discretion and sensitivity (Fisher, 2008). IAPT settings are different from other settings such as private practice partly due to their sheer size. Some IAPT services employ 70+ counsellors in addition to a number of managers, GPs and other health professionals. It is typically a requirement to record all client contact electronically. Moreover, since a lot of information gathering and communication takes place over the phone or via email, counsellors need to think about when and what details are appropriate to share with others. As a result of the Data Protection Act, clients have the right to request access to any information that has been recorded about them and there are also a number of professionals who may have access to this client information. This means that counsellors need to negotiate between maintaining client confidentiality and documenting information relevant to other health professionals. Furthermore, as a professional bound by an ethical framework, there may be times when confidentiality has to be broken to protect the safety of clients or the general public. Examples of this would include instances when clients disclose during counselling that they are planning to commit suicide or when there are evident child protection issues.

REFLECTION POINT

Conducting counselling in GP surgeries and mental health resource centres means that you have to share facilities with nurses, GPs and other medical staff. With regard to forming therapeutic relationships in such environments, contemplate the following issues.

- How do you think it might impact on your work as a counsellor to see clients in a room normally used by a GP, and at times their own GP's room?
- What, if any, additional considerations do you think would need to be given with regard to client confidentiality when working within a busy GP surgery or health centre?

CONDITIONS COMMONLY TREATED WITH IAPT

Problems such as depression, stress and general anxiety constitute a large proportion of the conditions treated within IAPT settings but are by no means exclusive to these services. However, it could be argued that some conditions are seen more frequently in IAPT in comparison with other counselling settings. One such condition is PTSD, which is characterised by the client having experienced a trauma during which their life or physical well-being was perceived as being under threat (e.g. car accidents, armed robbery, sexual assaults). Following the traumatic event, PTSD symptoms include: flashbacks, nightmares, panic attacks, intense anxiety, irritability and avoidance of stimuli with reference to the trauma experience (Rosen and Lilienfeld, 2008). PTSD is a condition that requires specific treatment protocols in order to avoid clients being re-traumatised.

Another condition frequently treated in IAPT settings is OCD. Clients suffering from OCD experience distressing thoughts, images or impulses (obsessions), such as being persistently frightened of being contaminated by bacteria or viruses. In order to reduce the anxiety and distress that these obsessions cause, the sufferer typically engages in particular rituals or habits (compulsions) such as, for example, excessive washing of hands or wearing rubber gloves all the time (Clark, 2007). Also treated in IAPT services are specific phobias such as emetophobia (fear of vomiting) and agoraphobia (fear of public places). Phobias are characterised by an intense and unrealistic fear of specific objects or situations that the person goes to great lengths to avoid. Phobias are often accompanied by panic attacks and it is a debilitating condition that significantly interferes with a person's everyday life (LeBeau et al., 2010).

Particular issues treated in IAPT are not limited to, but rather exemplified by the conditions outlined above. The variety of symptoms treated in IAPT settings can provide a dynamic, stimulating and varied work environment for counsellors, and potentially present counsellors with the opportunity to specialise in particular areas of interest. The multitude of presenting problems seen within the IAPT service does mean that counsellors need to work in a highly flexible manner and tailor their methods according to specific conditions and individual clients. It is also necessary to develop the knowledge and practical skills to treat a variety of conditions as well as being able to recognise those problems that may be outside one's competence or expertise.

CHAPTER SUMMARY

As we have learned in this chapter, the IAPT initiative was founded with the remit of addressing the shortfall of evidence-based psychological therapies in the treatment of depression and anxiety. The Layard report suggested that in order to improve mental health services in primary care there would need to be an established centrally led and government-funded framework that has the capacity to apply the NICE guidelines. The publication of this seminal report led to the launch of two IAPT demonstration sites in 2006, and the subsequent 11 Pathfinder sites. All of these sites were deemed largely successful, particularly in terms of the impressive number of people who engaged with the service. The most notable achievement was the service's ability in reaching out to social groups who previously had been poorly represented in the mental health framework. Clark et al.'s (2009) evaluation of the two demonstration sites highlighted the early success in making psychological therapies more accessible across local communities. In so doing, they indicated IAPT's potential in achieving one of its principal aims of improving access to psychological therapies for people suffering from depression and anxiety (Department of Health, 2008a).

Since the inception of IAPT, the service has continued to develop nationally, with over 100 PCTs becoming part of the IAPT initiative by the end of 2010. Working in compliance with the NICE guidelines is an integral part of the IAPT ethos, particularly in terms of applying evidence-based psychological therapies. The professional infrastructure of IAPT allows for these psychological therapies to be delivered within a stepped-care model, as recommended by the NICE guidelines. The essential principles of the stepped-care model outline the necessity to identify appropriate treatment for each individual client. With systematic reviews of the individual's progress and engagement, treatment can be specifically tailored and efficiently delivered by stepping up the intensity of care when necessary.

In fitting with the stepped-care model, the IAPT service has devised four main counselling roles. Working at step 3 of the stepped-care model are High Intensity Workers (HIWs) and High Intensity Trainees (HITs), who provide treatment for mild to severe depression and anxiety disorders within a CBT framework. Providing less intensive therapies at step 2 are Psychological Wellbeing Practitioners (PWPs) and PWP trainees. The focus for treatment at step 2 is on self-management and psycho-education rather than intensive psychological interventions, seen at higher steps.

As discussed earlier, working for IAPT in a counselling role offers various challenges and also a wide range of opportunities. The nature of IAPT means that counsellors predominately work autonomously, often in a fairly mobile capacity, seeing patients at more than one base on any given day. Working with a sense of independence challenges counsellors to network and build essential professional relationships with other healthcare professionals as well as third-party counselling services. These challenges have the potential to result in counsellors working in seeming isolation, which can be difficult for some. The challenges of working as a counsellor in this sector can also be extremely stimulating, varied and rewarding. It also places an emphasis on the individual counsellor to seek out the various opportunities available for their own personal and professional development.

Postscript: Since writing this chapter, the coalition government elected in May 2010 has set out proposals to change the way in which services are commissioned in the NHS. The outcome of these proposals for IAPT is not yet known but may alter the structures within which IAPT counsellors find themselves working in the future.

SUGGESTED FURTHER READING

Clark, D and Turpin, G (2008) Improving Opportunities. *The Psychologist,* 21(8): 700.

This paper discusses the different training opportunities for counsellors within the IAPT initiative.

Clark, DM, Layard, R, Smithies, R, Richards, DA, Suckling, R and Wright, B (2009) Improving Access to Psychological Therapy: Initial evaluation of two UK demonstration sites. *Behaviour Research and Therapy,* 47(11): 910–20.

Useful overview of how the IAPT initiative was initially implemented and conducted.

Ghosh, P (2009) Improving Access to Psychological Therapies for all Adults. *Psychiatric Bulletin,* 33(5): 186–8.

This text discusses some of the controversies surrounding the IAPT initiative in terms of its political and economical agenda.

Gunter, RW and Whittal, ML (2009) Dissemination of Cognitive-behavioral Treatments for Anxiety Disorders: Overcoming barriers and improving patient access. *Clinical Psychology Review,* 30(2): 194–202.

Approaches issues relevant to IAPT from a counselling and CBT perspective and how access into services can be made easier for clients.

ONLINE RESOURCES

www.babcp.com/ British Association for Behavioural and Cognitive Psychotherapies (BABCP).

www.bps.org.uk/ The British Psychological Society (BPS).

www.dh.gov.uk/en/index.htm Department of Health's website has several of the official papers outlining the implementation of the IAPT initiative.

www.iapt.nhs.uk NHS information site regarding the rollout of IAPT services.

References

Alcoholics Anonymous (2001) *Alcoholics Anonymous* (4th edition). New York: Alcoholics Anonymous World Services.

Armstrong, J (2010) How Effective are Minimally Trained/Experienced Volunteer Mental Health Counsellors? Evaluation of CORE Outcome Data. *Counselling & Psychotherapy Research*, 10(1): 22–31.

Association of University and College Counsellors (AUCC) (2004) *Recommended Framework of Good Practice for Counselling Services Working Within FE and HE Institutions*. Lutterworth: BACP.

Association of University and College Counsellors (AUCC) (2007) Know the Territory – An Overview of the UK Higher Education Arena. *AUCC Journal*, March 2007: 13–20.

Beck, AT (1991) Cognitive Therapy – A 30-year retrospective. *American Psychologist*, 46(4): 368–75.

Bell, E (1996) *Counselling in Further and Higher Education*. Buckingham: Open University Press.

Bennett, T (2000) *Drugs & Crime: The results of the second developmental stage of NEW-ADAM programme*. Home Office Online, www.homeoffice.gov.uk.

Beynon, CM et al. (2006) *Trends in Drop Out, Drug Free Discharge and Rates of Re-presentation: A retrospective cohort study of drug treatment clients in the North West of England*. Centre for Public Health, John Moores University, Liverpool. Available online at www.biomed central.com/1471–2458/6/205.

Bond, T and Jenkins, P (2008) Access to records of counselling and psychotherapy, BACP Information Sheet, G1. Lutterworth: BACP.

Boorman, S. (2009) NHS Health and Well-being, Final Report, November 2009. Available online at www.nhshealthandwellbeing.org/FinalReport.html

Bor, R (2002) *Counselling in Schools*. London: Sage.

British Association for Counselling and Psychotherapy (2001) *Good Practice for Counselling in Schools* (3rd edition) Rugby: BACP.

British Association for Counselling and Psychotherapy (2009) *Accreditation of Training Courses*. Lutterworth: BACP.

British Association for Counselling and Psychotherapy (2010) *Ethical Framework for Good Practice in Counselling and Psychotherapy* (Revised edition). Lutterworth: BACP.

Brooker, C, Repper, J, Beverley, C, Ferriter, M and Brewer, N (2002) *Mental Health Services and Prisoners: A review*. London: Department of Health. Available online at www.dh.gov.uk.

Bryant-Jefferies, R (2005) *Workplace Counselling in the NHS: Person-centred dialogues*. Abingdon: Radcliffe Publishing.

Burnside, J and Baker, N (2004) *Relational Justice, Repairing the Breach*. Winchester: Waterside Press.

Caleb, R (March 2010) The Roles Offered by Counselling Services in Further and Higher Education. *AUCC Journal*. Lutterworth: BACP.

Carroll, M (1996) *Workplace Counselling*. London: Sage.

Carroll, M and Walton, M (eds) (1997) *Handbook of Counselling in Organisations*. London: Sage.

Centre for Economic Performance at the London School of Economics (2006) *The Depression Report: A new deal for depression and anxiety disorders*. London: The London School of Economics and Political Science.

Claringbull, N (2010) *What is Counselling & Psychotherapy?* Exeter: Learning Matters.

Clark, DA (2007) *Cognitive Behavioural Therapy for OCD*. New York: The Guilford Press.

Clark, DM, Layard, R and Smithies, R (2008) *Improving Access to Psychological Therapy: Initial evaluation of the two demonstration sites. LSE Centre for Economic Performance Working Paper No. 1648*. London: London School of Economics. Available online at www.iapt.nhs.uk/wp-content/uploads/2008/09/lse-reports-final.pdf (accessed 12 March 2010).

Coates, J (2006) *No Big Deal. A Guide to Recovery from Addictions*. Norwich: Sow's Ear Press.

Cooper, M (2008) *Essential Research Findings in Counselling and Psychotherapy: The facts are friendly*. London: Sage.

Copeland, S (2005) *Counselling Supervision in Organisations: Professional and ethical dilemmas explored*. London: Routledge.

CSIP Choice and Access Team (2008) *Improving Access to Psychological Therapies (IAPT) Commissioning Toolkit*. Available online at www.dh.gov.uk/en/Publicationsandstatistics/Publications/PublicationsPolicyAndGuidance/DH_084065 (accessed 05/04/2010).

Department for Children, Schools and Families (2006) *Common Assessment Framework*. Available online at www.dcsf.gov.uk/everychildmatters/strategy/deliveringservices1/caf/cafframework/.

Department of Health (DH) (2007) *Commissioning a Brighter Future: Improving access to psychological therapies services*. London: The Stationery Office.

Department of Health (DH) (2007) *Trust, Assurance and Safety – The Regulation of Health Professionals in the 21st Century*. London: The Stationery Office.

Department of Health (DH) (2008a) *Improving Access for Psychological Therapies Implementation Plan: National guidelines for regional delivery*. London: The Stationery Office.

Department of Health (DH) (2008b) *Commissioning IAPT for the Whole Community: Improving access to psychological therapies*. London: The Stationery Office.

Donovan, DM and Marlatt, GA (1988) *Assessment of Addictive Behaviors*. New York: Guilford Press.

Elliott, R and Freire, E (2008) *Person-Centred/Experiential Therapies are Highly Effective: Summary of the 2008 meta-analysis*. Available online at www.bapca.co.uk/uploads/files/Meta-Summary091708.doc.

Fisher, MA (2008) Protecting Confidentiality Rights: The need for an ethical practice model. *American Psychologist*: 63(1), 1–13.

Franklin, L (2003) *An Introduction to Workplace Counselling*. Basingstoke: Palgrave Macmillan.

Gelard, K and Gelard, D (2009) *Counselling Adolescents* (3rd edition). London: Sage.

Ghosh, P (2009) Improving Access to Psychological Therapies for all Adults. *Psychiatric Bulletin*, 33(5): 186–88.

Gillick v West Norfolk Area Health Authority, House of Lords, 1985.

Grant, A (2009) Student services in the United Kingdom – an overview, in Osfield, KJ and Associates (eds) *The Internationalisation of Student Affairs and Services in Higher Education: An emerging global perspective*. Washington: NASPA.

Hanser, D, Scott, M and Braddock, A (2010) *Correctional Counselling*. New Jersey: Prentice-Hall.

Harris, B (2009) '"Extra appendage" or integrated service? School counsellors' reflection on their professional identity in an era of education reform"' *Counselling and Psychotherapy Research*, 9(3): 174–81.

Harvey, J and Smedley, K (2010) *Psychological Therapy in Prisons and Other Secure Locations*. Devon: Willan.

Health and Safety Executive (HSE) (2000) Securing Health Together. HSE Books. Available online at www.hse.gov.uk/sh2/sh2strategy.pdf

HM Government (2003) *Every Child Matters*. London: The Stationery Office. Available online at www.dcsf.gov.uk/everychildmatters/about/background

HM Government (2006) *Working Together to Safeguard Children: A guide to inter-agency working to safeguard and promote the welfare of children*. London: The Stationery Office. Available online at www.dcsf.gov.uk/everychildmatters/resources-and-practice/IG00060/.

HM Inspectorate of Prisons (2002) *Patient or Prisoner?* London: HMIP.

Hollanders, H (1999) Eclecticism and Integration in Counselling: Implications for training. *British Journal of Guidance & Counselling*, 27(4): 483–500.

Holloway, K and Bennett, T (2004) *The Results of the First Two Years of the NEW-ADAM Programme*. Home Office Online Report 19/04. Available online at www.homeoffice.gov.uk.

Home Office (2004) *British Crime Survey*. London: The Stationery Office.

Home Office (2007) *Sentencing Statistics 2005*. London: The Stationery Office.

Home Office Statistical Bulletin (2008) *Crime in England and Wales: Quarterly Update to September 2007*. Available online at www.homeoffice.gov.uk.

Hopkins, B (2004) *Just Schools: A whole school approach to restorative justice*. London: Jessica Kingsley Publishers.

Howerton, A, Byng, R, Campbell, J, Hess, D, Owens, C and Aitken, P (2007) Understanding Help-seeking Behaviour Among Male Offenders: a qualitative interview study. *British Medical Journal*, 334: 403.

Jones, A, Weston, S, Moody, A, Millar, T, Dollin, L, Anderson, T and Donmall, M (2007) *The Drug Treatment Outcomes Research Study: Baseline report*. London: The Home Office.

Johnston, H (ed) (2008) *Punishment and Control in Historical Perspective*. Basingstoke: Palgrave Macmillan.

Koch, C (1949/1952) *The Tree Test: The tree-drawing test as an aid to psychodiagnosis* (2nd edition). English Translation. Bern: H.Huber. Available online at www.daxcollection. org.au/docs/catalogue_ThreeTrees.pdf.

Kroenke, K, Spitzer, RL and Williams, JBW (2001) The PHQ-9: Validity of a brief depression severity measure. *Journal of General Internal Medicine*, 16(9): 606–13.

Kuyken, W, Padesky, CA and Dudley, R (2009) *Collaborative Case Conceptualization: Working effectively with clients in cognitive behavioural therapy*. New York: Guilford Press.

Labour Party Manifesto (2005) *Britain Forward not Back*. Available online at www.labour. org,uk.

LeBeau, RT, Glenn, D, Liao, B, Wittchen, H-U, Beesdo-Baum, K, Ollendick, T, et al. (2010) Specific Phobia: A review of DSM-IV specific phobia and preliminary recommendations for DSM-V. *Depression and Anxiety*, 27(2): 148–67.

Lenihan, P and Iliffe, S (2000) Counselling the Community: The contribution of counselling psychologists to the development of primary care. *Counselling Psychology Quarterly*, 13(4): 329-43.

Lloyd, M, Tysoe, E, Falshaw, L and Booth, S (2007) *The Mental Health of Prisoners: A thematic review of the care and support of prisoners with mental health needs*. London: HM Inspectorate of Prisons.

Löwe, B, Decker, O, Müller, S, Brähler, E, Schellberg, D, Herzog, W, et al. (2008) Validation and Standardization of the Generalized Anxiety Disorder Screener (GAD-7) in the General Population. *Medical Care*, 46(3): 266–74.

Margolin, A, Kleber, HD, Avants, SK, Konefal, J et al. (2002) Acupuncture for the Treatment of Cocaine Addiction: A randomized controlled trial. *Journal of the American Medical Association*, 287(1).

McLeod, J (1993) *An Introduction to Counselling*. Buckingham: Open University Press.

McLeod, J (2001; updated 2008) *Counselling in the Workplace: A Comprehensive Review of the Research Evidence*. Lutterworth: BACP.

Mearns, D (2004) *Counselling and Psychotherapy Workloads* BACP Information Sheet G4 (updated by Syme, G (2008) Lutterworth: BACP.

Morris, N and Rothman, D (eds) (1995) *The Oxford History of the Prison*. Oxford: Oxford University Press.

National Collaborating Centre for Mental Health (NCCMH) (co-published by the Royal College of Psychiatrists and the British Psychological Society) (2008) *Drug Misuse: Opioid Detoxification – The NICE Guidelines*. London: RCPsych Publications.

National Committee of Inquiry into Higher Education (1997) *Report of the National Committee*. Available online at www.leeds.ac.uk/educol/ncihe/.

National Institute for Health and Clinical Excellence (NICE) (2004) *Depression: Management of depression in primary and secondary care (CG23)*, superseded in 2009 by *Depression: The treatment and management of depression in adults (CG90)*. London: NICE. Available online at www.nice.org.uk/nicemedia/pdf/CG90NICEguideline.pdf.

National Treatment Agency (NTA) (2003) *Service Specification Tier 4: In-patient drug (and alcohol) misuse treatment*. Available online at www.nta.nhs.uk.

National Treatment Agency (NTA) (2006) *A Summary of the Review of Effectiveness of Treatment for Alcohol Problems*. Available online at www.nta.nhs.uk.

Nelson-Jones, R (2002) *Theory and Practice of Counselling and Therapy*. London: Continuum.

Newsome, A, Thorne, BJ, Wyld, K (1973) *Student Counselling in Practice*. London: University of London Press.

Norcross, JC and Goldfried, MR (2005) *Handbook of Psychotherapy Integration*. New York: OUP.

Norfolk Local Safeguarding Children's Board (2008). *A Guide to Inter-agency Working to Safeguard and Promote the Welfare of Children*. Available online at www.lscb.norfolk.gov.uk.

Norwich City College (2009) *Counselling Report 2008–09. Available online at* www.ccn.ac.uk.

Nuttall, J (2008) The Integrative Attitude – A personal journey. *European Journal of Psychotherapy and Counselling*, 10(1): 19–38.

Office for National Statistics (2010) *Statistical Bulletin: Suicide rates in the United Kingdom 1991–2008*. Available online at www.statistics.gov.uk.

Office of Public Sector Information (1998) *Data Protection Act 1998*. Available online at www.opsi.gov.uk/acts/acts1998.

Office of Public Sector Information (2001) *Special Educational Needs and Disability Act 2001*. Available online at www.opsi.gov.uk/ACTS/acts2001/ukpga_20010010_en_1.

O'Looney, S (2005) *Contexts of Counselling in Prison Setting: The case of young male prisoners affected by substance misuse*. Working Papers Series 4. Liverpool: Counselling Training Personal Development Consulting. Available online at www.ctpdc.co.uk.

Owers, A (2007) *Introduction: The mental health of prisoners: A thematic review of the care and support of prisoners with mental health needs*. London: HM Inspectorate of Prisons.

Phippen, M (2010) *Counselling in a Time of Change*. Unpublished presentation, 5 January. Cambridge.

Pollock, M (1998) *Counselling Women in Prison*. London: Sage.

Powell, DJ and Brodsky, A (2004) *Clinical Supervision in Alcohol and Drug Abuse Counselling*. San Francisco, CA: Jossey-Bass.

Prentiss, C (2006) *The Alcoholism and Addiction Cure – A holistic approach to total recovery*. Los Angeles, CA: Power Press.

Rawnsley, A (2010) *The End of the Party*. Harmondsworth: Penguin.

Reddy, M (1993) The Counselling Firmament: A short trip round the galaxy. *Counselling*, 4(1): 47–50. Lutterworth: BACP.

Rickford, D (2003) *Troubled Inside: Responding to the mental health needs of women in prison*. London: Prison Reform Trust. Available online at www.prisonreformtrust.org.uk.

Rickford, D and Edgar, K (2005) *Troubled Inside: Responding to the mental health needs of men in Prison*. London: Prison Reform Trust. Available online at www.prisonreformtrust.org.uk.

Robens Committee (1972) *Report of the Committee on Health and Safety at Work*. London, House of Commons: Parliamentary Report.

Rosen, GM and Lilienfeld, SO (2008) Posttraumatic Stress Disorder: An empirical evaluation of core assumptions. *Clinical Psychology Review*, 28(5): 837–68.

Rotman, E (1995) The Failure of Reform, in Morris & Rothman (Eds) *The Oxford History of the Prison*. Oxford: Oxford University Press.

Royal College of Psychiatrists (RCPsych) (2002) Working Party Report, *Suicide in Prisons, CR99*. London: Royal College of Psychiatrists.

Royal College of Psychiatrists (RCPsych) (2003) *The Mental Health of Students in Higher Education, CR112*. London: Royal College of Psychiatrists.

Schaeffer, B (1987) *Is it Love or Is It Addiction?* Minnesota: Hazeldon.

Smallwood, JA (2002) Counselling Psychology and the NHS: An individual perspective. *Counselling Psychology Review*, 17(1): 16–20.

Stewart, D (2008) *The Problems and Needs of Newly Sentenced Prisoners: Results from a national survey*. London: Ministry of Justice.

Sunderland, M (2008) *Draw on Your Emotions*. Milton Keynes: Speechmark Publishing.

Thorne, B (2008) *Infinitely Beloved*. London: Darton, Longman and Todd.

Thorsborne, M and Vinegrad, D (2009) *Restorative Justice Pocketbook*. Hampshire: Teacher's Pocketbooks.

Towl, G and Crighton, D (2002) Risk Assessment and Management, in Towl, G, Snow, L and McHugh, M (eds) *Suicide in Prisons*. Oxford: Wiley Blackwell.

Towl, G, Snow, L and McHugh, M (eds) (2002) *Suicide in Prisons*. Oxford: Wiley Blackwell.

Trower, P, Casey, A, and Dryden, W (2007) *Cognitive-behavioural Counselling in Action*. Thousand Oaks, CA: Sage.

Tyndall, N (1993) *Counselling in the Voluntary Sector*. Buckingham: Open University Press.

UK Council for International Student Affairs (2008) *International Students and Culture Shock*. Available online at www.ukcisa.org.uk/student/info_sheets/culture_shock.php.

UK Drug Policy Commission (UKDPC) (2008) *Reducing Drug Use, Reducing Reoffending*. London: UKDPC.

US Department of Health and Human Services (2005) *Substance Abuse Treatment: Group therapy – A treatment improvement protocol*. Rockville, MD: SAMHSA.

Useem, B (2008) *Prison State*. New York: Cambridge University Press.

Walsh, M (1998) (cited in O'Looney, S (2005) above) as What is Evidence? A critical view for nursing. *Clinical Effectiveness in Nursing*, 2: 86–93.

Whitfield, CL (1987) *Healing the Child Within*. Atlanta: Health Communications.

Winkelman, M (2003) Complementary Therapy for Addiction: Drumming out drugs. *American Journal of Public Health*, April, 93(4): 647–51.

World Health Organization (WHO) (2007) *The ICD-10 Classification of Mental and Behavioural Disorders Diagnostic Criteria for Research*. Geneva: World Health Organization.

Worsley, R (2007) *The Integrative Counselling Primer*. Herefordshire: PCCS Books.

Index